From Solomon to Malachi

From
Solomon to Malachi

KYLE M. YATES

Convention Press

NASHVILLE   TENNESSEE

Library of Congress Catalog Card Number: 59-9310

Printed in the United States of America
20. JUL 59 RRD

About the Author

KYLE MONROE YATES was born in Apex, North Carolina, the son of William Charles Manly and Della (Jones) Yates.

From Wake Forest College, North Carolina, he received the A.B. degree in 1916 and the A.M. in 1917. He received the Th.M. degree from Southern Baptist Seminary in 1920, the Th.D. from the same institution in 1922, and the Ph.D. from the University of Edinburgh in 1932.

He has been awarded a number of additional degrees: D.D. from Wake Forest College and from Mercer University in Georgia; LL.D. from Union University in 1939; and Litt. D. from Baylor University, Waco, Texas, in 1948.

Dr. Yates was ordained to the gospel ministry in 1916. He has held pastorates at Fort Barnwell, North Carolina; New Castle, Kentucky; and New Salem, Kentucky. He has also served as pastor of Beechmont Baptist Church and Walnut Street Baptist Church, Louisville, Kentucky, and Second Baptist Church, Houston, Texas.

He was professor of Old Testament at Southern Baptist Theological Seminary 1922–42, and is now distinguished professor of Bible at Baylor University. Since 1938 he has been a member of the committee on the revision of the Old Testament.

In August, 1922, Dr. Yates married Margaret Webb Sharp. They have three children: Kyle M., Margaret Jean, and Ellen.

Dr. Yates is the author of a number of books: *A Beginner's Grammar of the Hebrew Old Testament, Essentials of Biblical Hebrew, Preaching from the Prophets, Preaching from the Psalms, Preaching from Great Bible Chapters, Studies in the Psalms,* and FROM SOLOMON TO MALACHI.

44778

Contents

Church Study Course for Teaching and Training

THE CHURCH STUDY COURSE for Teaching and Training began October 1, 1959. It is a merger of three courses previously promoted by the Sunday School Board—the Sunday School Training Course, the Graded Training Union Study Course, and the Church Music Training Course.

The course is fully graded. The system of awards provides a series of five diplomas of twenty books each for Adults or Young People, one diploma of ten books for Young People, two diplomas of five books each for Intermediates, and two diplomas of five books each for Juniors. Book awards earned previously in the Sunday School Training Course, the Graded Training Union Study Course, and the Church Music Training Course may be transferred to the new course.

The course is comprehensive, with books grouped into nineteen categories. The purpose of the course is to (1) help Christians to grow in knowledge and conviction; (2) help them grow toward maturity in Christian character and competence for service; (3) encourage them to participate worthily as workers in their churches; and (4) develop leaders for all phases of church life.

The Church Study Course for Teaching and Training is promoted by the Baptist Sunday School Board, 127 Ninth Avenue, North, Nashville, Tennessee, through its Sunday School, Training Union, Church Music, and Church Administration departments, and by these same departments in the states affiliated with the Southern Baptist Convention. A complete description of the course and the system of awards may be found in the *Church Study Course for Teaching and Training* catalog which may be obtained without charge from any one of these departments.

A record of all awards earned should be maintained in each church. A person should be designated by the church to keep the files. Forms for such records may be ordered from any Baptist Book Store.

Requirements for Credit in Class
or Home Study

IF CREDIT is desired for the study of this book in a class or by home study, the following requirements must be met:

I. In Classwork

1. The class must meet a minimum of seven and one-half clock hours. The required time does not include assembly periods. Ten class periods of forty-five minutes each are recommended. (If laboratory or clinical work is desired in specialized or technical courses, this requirement may be met by six clock hours of classwork and three clock hours of supervised laboratory or clinical work.)

2. A class member who attends all class sessions and completes the reading of the book within a week following the last class session will not be required to do any written work.

3. A class member who is absent from one or more sessions must answer the questions on all chapters he misses. In such a case, he must turn in his paper within a week and must certify that the book has been read.

4. The teacher should request an award for himself. A person who teaches a book in sections B, C, or D of any category or conducts an approved unit of instruction for Nursery, Beginner, or Primary children will be granted an award in category 11, Special Studies, which will count as an elective on his own diploma. He should specify in his request the name of the book taught, or the unit conducted for Nursery, Beginners, or Primaries.

5. The teacher should complete the Request for Book Award— Class Study (Form 150) and forward it within two weeks after the completion of the class to the Church Study Course Awards Office, 127 Ninth Avenue, North, Nashville 3, Tennessee.

II. In Home Study

1. A person who does not attend any class session may receive credit by answering all questions for written work as indicated in the book. When a person turns in his paper on home study, he must certify that he has read the book.

2. Students may find profit in studying the text together, but individual papers are required. Carbon copies or duplicates in any form cannot be accepted.

3. Home study work papers may be graded by the pastor or a person designated by him, or they may be sent to the Church Study Course Awards Office for grading. The form Request for Book Award—Home Study (Form 151) must be used in requesting awards. It should be mailed to Church Study Course Awards Office, 127 Ninth Avenue, North, Nashville 3, Tennessee.

III. CREDIT FOR THIS BOOK

This book is No. 0204 in category 2, section A.

Suggested Audio-Visual Materials

For Use in Teaching This Book

THE FOLLOWING LIST of audio-visual materials will be helpful in teaching this book. In some instances more material is listed than it will be practical to use. In such cases, select the frames of the filmstrips and portions of motion pictures that contribute most directly to the chapters of the book and that are best related to your teaching purpose and to the specific needs of the group you are teaching.

CHAPTER 1
> Slides: N 67 *Solomon Anointed King;* N 69 *Solomon Judging His People;* N 70 *Solomon Dedicating the Temple*
> Motion Picture: *Solomon, a Man of Wisdom*

CHAPTER 2
> Slides: Ha 61 *Rehoboam Accepts Counsel of the Young Man;* N 72 *The Kingdom Torn Asunder;* N 74 *Asa's Covenant*

CHAPTER 3
> Slides: N 75 *Elijah and the Ravens;* Ha 62 *Elijah and the Prophets of Baal;* N 80 *Elijah and Ahab in Naboth's Vineyard;* Ha 81 *Elijah Taken up to Heaven*
> Motion Picture: *Elijah, a Fearless Prophet*

CHAPTER 4
> Slide: N 90 *Jonah at Nineveh*

CHAPTER 5
> Slide: N 91 *Amos the Fearless Prophet*
> Filmstrip: *Amos and Hosea*

CHAPTER 6
> Slides: Ha 694 *Hezekiah's Passover;* Ha 695 *Hezekiah's Prayer in the Temple*

CHAPTER 7

Slides: N 101 *Josiah Hearing the Words of the Law;* Ha 700 *Shaphan Reads the Book of the Law to Josiah;* Ha 702 *Jeremiah Rescued from the Mob;* Ha 703 *Jeremiah Saved by King Zedekiah*

CHAPTER 8

Slides: Ha 704 *Daniel and His Friends Refuse Meat and Wine;* Ha 708 *Daniel's Prayer;* Ha 698 *Ezekiel Warns the Jewish People*
Filmstrip: *Daniel in the Lions' Den*
Motion Picture: *Daniel in the Lions' Den*

CHAPTER 9

Slides: Ha 64 *Cyrus Befriends the Captive Jews;* Ha 715 *Dedication of the Walls*
Filmstrips: *Ezra; Nehemiah* (Old Testament History Prophets)

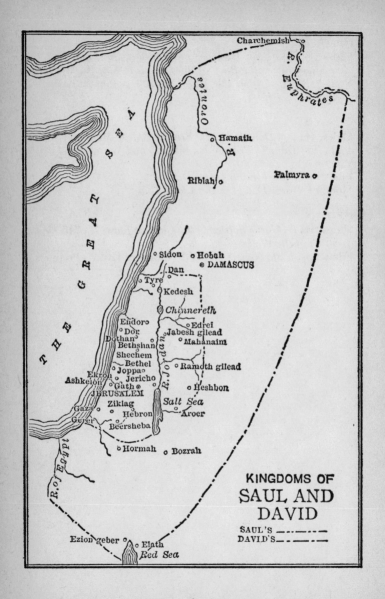

KINGDOMS OF
SAUL AND
DAVID

SAUL'S ———————
DAVID'S —·—·—·—

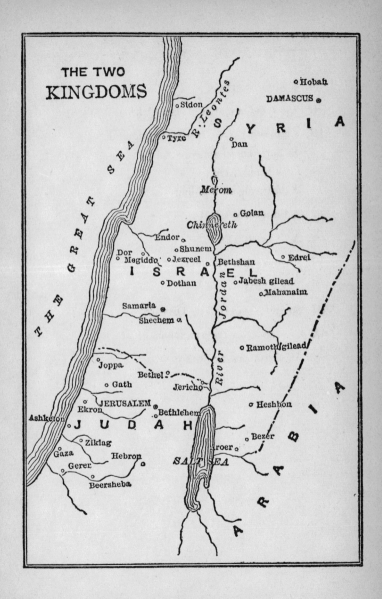

THE TWO
KINGDOMS

THE GREAT SEA

Sidon

R. Leontes

Tyre

SYRIA

Hobah

DAMASCUS

Dan

Merom

Chinnereth

Golan

Endor

Shunem

Dor

Megiddo

Jezreel

Bethshan

Edrei

ISRAEL

Dothan

Jabesh gilead

Mahanaim

Samaria

Shechem

River Jordan

Ramoth gilead

Joppa

Bethel

Gath

Jericho

JERUSALEM

Ekron

Bethlehem

Heshbon

Ashkelon

JUDAH

Ziklag

Bezer

Gaza

Aroer

Gerer

Hebron

SALT SEA

Beersheba

ARABIA

XV

CHAPTER 1

1

SOLOMON

1 Kings 1–11; 2 Chronicles 1–9

THE THIRD KING over God's chosen nation, Solomon came to the throne under most advantageous conditions.

I. A RICH HERITAGE

Solomon came into the place of power and authority with the proverbial silver spoon between his teeth. His father David and his mother Bathsheba made it possible for him to begin life well ahead of the procession. Saul had failed, but David succeeded in a marvelous way. The court of David was a great place for the young prince to live and grow.

The enemies of God's people had been gradually driven back and subdued. The boundaries of the kingdom had been pushed back until David reigned over a respectable kingdom. God was smiling upon the country in an unmistakable way. Because of David's wisdom and popularity, the kingdom was united and the people engaged in friendly work together. It was an era of prosperity, peace, and plenty.

David was a devout worshiper of Jehovah and had developed the religious life of the kingdom to a very high plane. Strong emphasis had been placed on sacred music

1

and public worship. Solomon found a strong emphasis on worship and godliness.

His kingdom was not only at peace with all the world, but friendly alliances with neighboring kingdoms made material prosperity inevitable. Hiram, king of Tyre, was a staunch friend who was able to make Solomon rich. The stupendous building program was practically assured by such alliances.

David had carried in his inner heart a dream of a beautiful temple for God. The blueprints and specifications called for a magnificent building to the glory of Jehovah of hosts. Although he was forbidden to build, the old king gathered rich stores of materials and money that the Temple might be assured. A conservative estimate places the value of two and one-half billion dollars on the sum left to Solomon.

The young king was endowed with kingly blood, the favor and approval of God, the blessings of David his father, the universal acclaim of his people, a united and happy nation, and every other evidence of the smile of heaven upon him.

II. An Auspicious Beginning (1 Kings 3:4-15)

In the early days of his reign, Solomon met God and was deeply impressed by the experience. In God's presence he acknowledged his great debt to his father and to God. He confessed his own weakness and lack of experience. He knew that he could not carry on the work of the kingdom in his own strength. In the deep consciousness of his need, he requested of God an understanding heart that he might know how to guide the destinies of the kingdom. It was a noble prayer. He wanted wisdom to represent God in the affairs of the kingdom.

Jehovah was delighted with Solomon and his request. Nothing could have pleased God more. He realized that the young man might have asked for long life, riches, the life of his enemies, or a number of other selfish things. In accordance with the divine nature, God gave Solomon the desire of his heart and added many other things. God always stands ready to give more than we ask.

With such a beginning, surely the young Solomon must reach heights never before scaled by one of God's representatives! It seems too good to be true to find such a fine spirit of reverence, humility, gratitude, and obedience in a ruler.

III. GROWING POWER AND MAGNIFICENCE

Out of such promising beginnings there developed a period when the united kingdom under Solomon reached its golden age. Yet seeds of decay were developing in the midst of pomp and glory.

1. *Early Developments*

It did not take long for Solomon to demonstrate to the world that he was to be the autocratic ruler of his realm. He had very little sympathy with the democratic aspirations of his people. It was easy to see that he planned to be an Oriental despot. Each man who gave any evidence of being in his way was put aside. Adonijah, his older brother, had attempted to seize the throne before the death of David. He was considered dangerous and, on a rather flimsy pretext, was executed by the order of Solomon.

Abiathar, the priest, and Joab, the chief of the army, were quickly deposed. The priest was banished and Joab was brutally executed. Shimei, who had cursed David, was killed to make the way safe for Solomon.

In order to insure political strength, Solomon took the daughter of Pharaoh as one of his wives. It was a shrewd move on his part to guarantee Egyptian support. He seemed to ignore the dangers that were involved. He was bent on having a great kingdom.

2. A Magnificent Court

It had already been evident that Solomon was headed for a rich, secular, worldly, magnificent, Oriental court. He believed that his city and his court should rival all others. Luxury was the one order of the day.

The ambitious king felt that he must have beautiful palaces, strong walls, plenty of soldiers, luxurious furnishings, and all that went with the Oriental court. We are told that he presented such a dazzling array of fine things that the Queen of Sheba was practically "knocked breathless" before him. It was more than she was prepared to see. When we consider that she had probably been accustomed to a fine display of magnificent furnishings herself, we are more impressed with the implications of her tribute.

Women from all the neighboring countries were brought in, until Solomon's harem was full of carefully selected beauties. They, of course, added to the picture a note of luxury, abandon, and show. The total number of these women was one thousand.

Trade routes were opened and heavy tolls were taken of all traders. Solomon's kingdom lay on the bridge between the great world kingdoms. It was easy to exact tribute from all of the caravans.

By using the Phoenicians, Israel's king was able to build and operate a great fleet of trading vessels. These boats brought back fabulous treasures from all the Eastern markets. The gold, jewels, fine garments, spices, and other precious wares only added to the splendor and magnificence of his worldly kingdom. The staggering totals of his wealth are almost beyond belief.

3. *Extravagant Building*

It was as a builder that the young king left enduring monuments. The erection of the Temple on Mount Moriah was the outstanding event of his reign. That structure became the one unifying force in the kingdom.

The famous old mountain was redolent with memories of Abraham, Isaac, and David. On that sacred spot David had planned to build a beautiful house for God. For years he had looked to the hill for the fulfilment of his dreams. Valuable material, supplies, and money were gathered and made ready for the structure.

Solomon took the specifications from his father's hands, gathered up the materials, called Hiram of Tyre into the deal, and set out to do God's bidding with all his heart. The hill was leveled and filled in until an area of about twelve acres was prepared.

The treasures of the world were ransacked for wood, stone, metal, and fine things. The cedars of Lebanon were purchased, cut, prepared, transported to the sea, floated down to the spot nearest Jerusalem, carried up the steep mountain to the city, and put in their places according to the plans.

Solomon adopted the Egyptian method of using forced labor. His own people, as well as the Canaanites, were included in the draft. However, they were not made actual slaves (1 Kings 9:22). Thirty thousand men labored in the mountains of Lebanon. He used seventy thousand to carry the logs up the steep hill. Eighty thousand men were forced to work in the quarries (1 Kings 5:13–16). Cruel taskmasters were employed to drive the workers to their utmost.

Even with this army of workers the task of building the Temple required more than seven years. Hiram of Tyre furnished the skilled workmen who became responsible for the actual completion of the work.

The Temple was built on the same plan used in the construction of the tabernacle except that it was made twice as large. It was probably about one hundred and twenty feet by sixty feet. Even though it was not a large structure, it was one of the finest and most famous buildings ever erected on the earth. God's name was honored by the splendor of the house of worship.

After the completion of the Temple, the army of workers labored for thirteen years to complete the king's great palace. The same fine materials were used, and the luxurious furnishings were brought to make the palace a beautiful one.

In addition to these two buildings, Solomon built a magnificent palace for his Egyptian wife, six cities, an armory, supply depots for the army, and pools and walls on every hand. It was a real program of public works that left the people gasping when they looked upon the evidences of wealth and splendor.

IV. A FOOLISH WISE MAN

The wisdom of Solomon was a special gift from God. At Gibeon he had been granted such extraordinary powers that he became the wisest man of his age. As a judge and executive he had no equal in the land. He had prayed for an understanding heart that he might be able to judge the people wisely and intelligently. That wisdom had been given, so that his fame as a wise man spread far and wide. His quick, ready wit and his keen, alert mind brought him standing as the wisest of the wise.

This wisdom was strictly limited in its scope. Solomon failed to show evidences of sympathy, tolerance, tact in handling his people, and wisdom in dealing with poor, stricken subjects. He was vain and ungodly in his desires for material gain and outward show. He became a reckless spender and a lover of vain display. His one thousand wives and concubines ruined him. He could not be counted wise after such a foolish venture as was manifested in the collection of women from all the surrounding peoples.

After his complete surrender to worldly things, Solomon ceased to show the proper love for Jehovah. He could not worship God with devotion and at the same time pay homage to all the gods of the heathen peoples. His desire to please the neighboring peoples by bowing down to their gods was a foolish move.

Perhaps one of the most apparent evidences of lack of wisdom was Solomon's utter disregard of the rights of the people when he needed money or work. His people merely existed to make possible the full gratification of every desire of the king. If he wanted a hundred thousand workmen for his building program, he forced them to go to work. Tribute money and taxes were taken from the people in such quantities that very little was left. The cruel taxgatherers robbed the people of practically everything they possessed. The ambitious king failed to realize that he was literally destroying the morale and spirit of his subjects. How he was able to keep down actual revolts and uprisings is more than we can explain. God was watching over the foolish one.

V. A GREAT RULER

In spite of these serious defects and mistakes, Solomon has been classed among the great rulers. He was foolish, but the forty years of his reign saw a tremendous growth in many directions. It was an era of prosperity, peace, expansion, building, fortification, extension of trade and commerce, alliance with the other peoples, and forward movements along many lines. His public works program provided many public buildings and fortifications that made for security, unification, and power. Solomon contributed much to his kingdom. He will always be placed among the great rulers in Jerusalem. His efforts in the direction of permanent peace for his land constituted a real contribution. "And Judah and Israel dwelt safely, every man under his vine and under his fig tree, . . . all the days of Solomon" (1 Kings 4:25).

VI. REVOLTS AND TROUBLE

Damascus, in the north, and Edom, in the south, soon showed signs of revolt. These peoples were not satisfied to be under the yoke of Solomon. It was an easy matter to break away from him and declare their independence. The ruler in each of these lands carved off a generous slice of the land controlled by Solomon. There was a marked indication of weakness as each crisis came upon the king whose reign had begun with such promise.

A more serious test came when Jeroboam led an active movement against the king. Jeroboam had been one of Solomon's trusted overseers and had been given a real opportunity to know and cultivate the friendship of the people. He knew how to offer sympathy and to listen to their cries of woe. He conceived the idea that he could serve his people better by a definite revolt. He decided to call out the people of the northern part of the country and break away from the authority of Solomon.

The move came very near being serious for the country. Solomon was able to put it down, and Jeroboam was forced to flee to Egypt to save his life. He realized that the victory could be his on the death of the king. He was waiting for the day when he could go forth to deliver his people from the cruel taskmaster. Shishak of Egypt was glad to welcome and protect Jeroboam in his palace. The young rebel continued his close touch with the Northern tribes until the death of Solomon.

We may be sure that the king's last days were not happy ones. The consequences of his sins were heavier than he had imagined. The wealth, position, prominence, knowledge, wisdom, wives, concubines, horses, chariots, soldiers, buildings, cities, trade routes, and victories, failed to bring real happiness. The reign that had started in such a blaze of glory and had continued to be more illustrious with each passing year, at last lost much of its glamour and grandeur. Solomon realized that he had failed.

VII. THE CRISIS

When news reached Egypt of the death of Solomon, the young Jeroboam was ready to start instantly. The Northern tribes would be waiting for him to lead them in revolt. All the tribes had been willing to accept David's choice of Solomon some forty years before, but they were not ready for such dictation now in their choice of a king.

Rehoboam took up the affairs of the kingdom and declared himself king of the whole land. When met by a bold demand to reverse his father's policies, he was not equal to the emergency. It was more than he could handle. The people of the North were demanding that excessive taxation and forced labor be lessened and made more reasonable. They made it perfectly clear that real trouble was ahead if the young king failed to adjust the burdens. It was a challenge.

Rehoboam was a very foolish young man and failed utterly in his first great crisis. Contrary to the counsel of his old advisers, he angered the delegates with a bitter promise to add to the burdens and rough treatment. He made revolt absolutely necessary.

It was the hour for which Jeroboam had waited. The people were so inflamed by the insolent treatment that they were ready for anything. They were at white heat. With the old war cry of Sheba they yelled: "What portion have we in David? neither have we inheritance in the son of Jesse: to your tents, O Israel: now see to thine own house, David" (1 Kings 12:16). Thus the greater part of the kingdom was in open revolt and Rehoboam was left alone with a small handful of followers.

The chief overseer of forced labor was sent by Rehoboam to put down the rebellion and save the kingdom.
He was probably hated as much as any man in the kingdom. Instant death was his portion. The people of the
North were enraged enough to do anything.

Jeroboam, who had been keeping himself behind the
scene rather effectively, now came forth to assume leadership of the ten tribes. At ancient Shechem he was
solemnly anointed king over Israel. He was to rule in
the North (Israel), and Rehoboam could keep his little
kingdom (Judah) in the South. Secession was in effect.
The kingdom was split and ruined. Jeroboam's ambition
had finally been realized, and the mighty kingdom of
David and Solomon was no more. The city of Jerusalem
with the Temple was left with the kingdom of Judah.

VIII. Some Causes of the Division

Several things may be put down as causes of the serious revolt and division:

1. An old jealousy that dated back to the days of the
judges caused constant uneasiness among the people.

2. Solomon's apostasy and his worship of idols served
to cause the finer religious element to lose faith in him
and to allow their devotion to cool. The people turned
away from Jehovah to serve the gods of the Moabites and
the Zidonians.

3. The heavy burden of taxation and forced labor
broke the spirit of the people and caused them to be
bitter in their resentment. This terrific drain of men and
money was especially serious in the eyes of the men of
the North. They were being robbed of their liberty to

build a city in the southern part of the land and keep up
the court of a king whom they despised.

4. The selfish ambition of Jeroboam led him to stir up
hatred and revolt among the people of the North. It was
comparatively easy to cause trouble among people who
were so sorely oppressed. Jeroboam used his opportunity.

5. The incredible shortsightedness of the foolish Rehoboam was the immediate cause. In the face of such foolish treatment, division was inevitable.

IX. Consequences of the Division

A new order came into being. Instead of one united,
powerful kingdom under the iron hand of a despotic dictator, there were now two weak kingdoms constantly at
war with each other and attacked from all sides by foes
who made bold to assert themselves. Jeroboam in the
North had three times as many people, five times as
much territory, a more fertile soil, much better military
equipment, and a wide-open area not so easily defended.
The people of the North were shut off from the Temple
and from all religious observance except as Jeroboam ar-
ranged. He took pains to start it with golden calves and a
priesthood made of volunteers from any of the people.
The Levites left his borders and flocked to Jerusalem,
thus leaving his land devoid of fervent worshipers of
Jehovah.

Rehoboam in the South did not have much territory or
many people, but he had Jerusalem and the holy sanctuary. The city had enjoyed the greater part of the fruits
of Solomon's building craze. There was more spiritual
power in Judah.

The Northern Kingdom (Israel) lasted for 209 years,

with nineteen kings sitting on its throne before it was swept away into exile by the great Assyrian monarch (Sargon II). These kings were all bad in the sense that they did not worship and follow Jehovah. Some of them ruled well from a worldy point of view, but not one of them was able to do anything for Jehovah. Prophets preached to them and God ministered to them, but they continued to sin to the end.

The Southern Kingdom (Judah) continued for 344 years,[1] with nineteen kings sitting on the throne in Jerusalem before it was taken into exile by Nebuchadnezzar, the king of Babylon. Several of Judah's kings were pious, fervent worshipers of Jehovah and succeeded in drawing the people back to God. The faithful prophets preached and brought special messages from God for each crisis.

It was a dark day, though, when the mighty kingdom of David and Solomon was broken up and weakened. However, God's hand was still guiding the destinies of his people, and he could bring order out of chaos and victory out of defeat.

X. An Estimate of Solomon

For forty years Solomon was able to hold together the great kingdom that David had built up by years of warfare. It took an iron hand and a keen mind to do it. God gave him the wisdom and the power to continue. Surrounding nations were either beaten off or kept in line by diplomatic alliances.

Solomon was a statesman and a diplomat as well as a dictator. His contribution to the transformation of a rough military stronghold into the most beautiful city of the land was a real accomplishment. By means of the

Temple he gave new dignity and beauty to the worship of Jehovah. His court became one of the wonders of the world.

Under his influence, art and literature flourished. He was responsible for writing or collecting many of the fine teachings included in our Bible. The Hebrew nation came into a place of importance among the nations of the world. Solomon's fine business ability made possible a stream of money and gems that flowed in from all directions. Prosperity, luxury, peace, and splendor characterized his reign.

When one looks beneath the surface he is impressed with the reality of disintegrating forces that were at work. Slowly but surely the despotic king was destroying the enthusiam, loyalty, and affection of his subjects. Enslavement, exorbitant taxes, and lack of sympathy for his people were breaking down all the spirit of love and loyalty that should have been evident on every hand. Solomon's pride and ungodly ambition for display led him into an orgy of reckless spending that practically wrecked the country.

Immoral and pagan practices introduced into his court put an end to religious fervor, and God's smile of approval was turned away. Solomon lacked the stamina to stand for the faith of his father and to keep the religion of Jehovah clean before the people.

It had been easy, under God's hand, to climb the heights to success. The young king's faith in God, his courage, wisdom, and brilliance, led him to the heights; but he failed miserably when he forgot God and turned to follow his own mad desires. He lacked the solid char-

acter to hold the forts he had won. When he died the
inevitable crash came.

FOR CLASS DISCUSSION AND FURTHER STUDY

1. Do you consider Solomon's life on the whole as successful or
   unsuccessful? What are your reasons for your conclusions?
2. Why did Solomon, after his experience at Gibeon (1 Kings
   3 : 4–15), still do so many foolish things? What word of warning for all of us seems to be implied in his experience?
3. List the factors which ultimately caused the decline in the
   kingdom which had been Solomon's. Cite instances of other
   nations which have been undermined by similar forces. This
   point may lead to some research, and some earnest consideration of conditions in our own land.

---

[1] Not all Bible scholars agree exactly on chronology, and some varia-
tions will be noted between dates given in the body of this book and
those in the chart on page 55. Since there were several deportations, the
exact date to use for the beginning of the exile is difficult to set.

CHAPTER 2

2

EARLY DAYS OF
THE DIVIDED KINGDOM

1 Kings 12–16; 2 Chronicles 10–12

THE REVOLT of the Northern tribes ushered in a long period in the history of God's people during which two kingdoms existed side by side.

I. RIVAL KINGDOMS

The ten tribes in the North under Jeroboam took with them the name "Israel." That had been the name of David's kingdom and it seems that the seceding tribes should have used a different name, leaving the old name with Rehoboam at Jerusalem. Jeroboam believed in having his own way in such matters, and so his kingdom was called "Israel" while Rehoboam's was called "Judah." From 931 B.C. to 722 B.C., these kingdoms existed side by side. During a great part of this time they were fighting with each other and calling in cruel enemies to help wage the war when the going was rough.

II. JEROBOAM'S RELIGIOUS ZEAL

We may not think of Jeroboam as a man interested in religion, but one of the first things he did was to set up places of worship for his people. We will certainly not approve of the form of worship he made available, but he was anxious to do his part toward giving his people something to worship. His first move was to see that his newly established capital was fortified. He also prepared Penuel, across the Jordan, as a place of safety in time of danger. Since Rehoboam was making war against him, the rebel king was forced to put forth his best efforts in defense.

Jeroboam set up a sanctuary at Dan in the far North and one at Bethel in the extreme South. In each of these sanctuaries he put up the image of a golden bull which, in Semitic religions, was a common symbol of the deity. Aaron had made calves of gold for the wanderers to worship. These calves symbolized the god of the storm and of vegetation. Jeroboam seems to have been anxious to have the people worship Jehovah by means of these idols. He was ignorant and unable to appreciate the true spiritual concepts. He had no beautiful temple in his domain. He did not see any need of such a building. He provided means so that his subjects could reach one of these sanctuaries and worship God.

Jeroboam was anxious to satisfy his people so that they would not attempt to go all the way to Jerusalem to worship. He sought to keep them away from Jerusalem. He could not hope to build up a great kingdom if his people had to go to another land to worship.

In his efforts to win the people, Jeroboam selected priests from the ranks without any regard for the Levites. This resulted in the withdrawing of many of his best people, who went to live in Judah. It also meant that the worship in the North was increasingly secular, idolatrous, and ungodly. The king was more of a warrior and politician than a representative of God in religious matters. The religion of the North reverted to Canaanite paganism. It was a fatal step that launched the kingdom on the toboggan toward ruin.

III. REHOBOAM A WEAK RULER

Early in his career it was made clear that Rehoboam (Solomon's son) was a weakling. In his foolish mistake he lost nearly all of the great kingdom built up by his father and grandfather. Benjamin held to Judah and the city of Jerusalem was in his territory. He had the Temple, and the Levites flocked to him.

During all of his seventeen years, Rehoboam continued to fight with his brothers of the North. When Jeroboam was driven across the Jordan, he called in his friend Shishak of Egypt, who administered a stinging defeat to Rehoboam. In order to save his city, he was forced to bring out all the Temple treasures and all his wealth to buy off the thirsty Pharaoh. It was a serious blow to the hopes of Rehoboam. He did not invade the land of Israel after this overthrow, but continued to defend his own land.

IV. THE GOOD REIGN OF ASA IN JUDAH

The early days in a corrupt court might have spelled ruin for the young king Asa, but we find him much better than his immediate ancestors. The wars had practically ceased when he came to the throne. It was clear to him that his people were not true to God. Too many idols and idol furniture were visible. It took real courage to begin cleaning up the land. The "pillars," "obelisks," "asherim," "sun images," and "high places" were torn down and destroyed. Such relics of heathenism had no place in Jehovah's land.

Asa's next step was in the direction of building walls, cities, towers, gates, armies, and the kingdom. He believed in preparedness and, even though he was not engaged in a war in his early days, he was doing his best to be ready for the coming clouds.

When Zerah, the Ethiopian, came against Asa with his million soldiers, the outlook was dark. Judah's little army was trained, equipped, and ready; but what could they hope to do against so many? In answer to earnest prayer, Jehovah came to the rescue and helped the brave soldiers of Asa win a great victory. It was a glorious triumph for God's forces.

On the way home, the victorious army was met by an inspired preacher from God, who assured them that they could continue to win victories as long as they were willing to rely upon Jehovah. He reminded them of God's help in the ages past and of his promises for the future. It was a good time for the king to continue his reforms and to put out every vestige of idolatry and heathenism from the land.

The young king, Asa, accepted the challenge and enlisted his army in a vigorous crusade against idolatry, vice, false practices, and heathen cults. They seemed to fight with the same enthusiasm that they had manifested in the battle against Zerah.

Following the breaking down of all objectionable idol furniture, Asa called the people together for a solemn meeting. Sacrifices were offered and a sacred covenant was made with God. The people were deeply impressed and shouted aloud their vows of allegiance to God. It was a high day in Zion. It seemed that Jehovah's name was to be honored throughout the entire land again.

War clouds appeared again as Baasha, the king of Israel, came against Asa. It was a serious crisis for Judah. The one who had won a victory from the great army of Ethiopia was not equal to the test, and curled up from fright when attacked by Baasha. Asa resorted to a short-sighted expedient when he called in the army of the Syrians (Damascus) to attack the hosts of Baasha from the rear. The Syrian king was only too glad to take advantage of the opportunity. It gave him a secure hold on all the land. God was sorely displeased with the lack of faith of his king in Judah and sent a preacher with a sharp rebuke.

After a long life Asa died of gout. Instead of calling upon God for help in his trouble, he appealed to the native healers who used incantations and adjurations. Asa had done much for his kingdom, but some of his policies were exceedingly foolish. He failed in refusing to trust Jehovah.

V. Jehoshaphat of Judah

Asa's son carried on the good work started by his father. His reign was one of unusual religious activity. Jehoshaphat seemed anxious to consult Jehovah on every occasion. He wanted guidance for every step of his career and openly called on God for the manifestation of his favor. The national worship was purified and made beautiful.

Jehovah blessed the godly king and gave him "riches and honor in abundance." For twenty-five years he led his people into better living and finer citizenship. He inaugurated a system of public instruction for the entire land. A commission composed of priests, Levites, and princes was appointed to tour the country and teach the people. We do not know how many teachers were used or how long the work continued, but we may be certain that much good was accomplished in ridding his land of ignorance. The book of the Law was the textbook used.

Jehoshaphat built castles, cities, walls, and strong fortifications throughout his territory, and developed his army to a high standing. Judges were appointed to settle difficulties in every locality. It was his aim to make possible a more efficient administration of justice.

It seems that Jehoshaphat was able to control the surrounding nations and collect tribute from them. For the first time since the break at the death of Solomon, peace was made with the inhabitants of the North. Jehoshaphat cultivated Ahab, the king of Israel, and an alliance was effected that put an end to the bitter warfare. The daughter of Ahab and Jezebel was given in marriage to Jehoram the son of Jehoshaphat. They thought that union would work wonders for the two nations. It practically ruined Judah later, because this woman, Athaliah, brought over into Judah her Baal worship, and soon the religious stream was muddy from the introduction of this vile element. The advantage gained politically and materially was more than counterbalanced by this serious invasion of Baalism. Dark days loomed for the people of Jerusalem. Jehoshaphat died at the age of sixty, leaving his throne to Jehoram, the young husband of Athaliah.

VI. TROUBLOUS DAYS IN ISRAEL

Following the death of Jeroboam in the North, his son Nadab came to the throne. It soon became evident that the control of the state was not to be in the hands of the civilian population, but in the hands of the military class. The army faction that happened to have control used the power to put in its candidate for the leadership of the country. Poor Nadab lasted only two years. An ambitious army officer named Baasha was as unscrupulous as he was bold, and murder was easy. The dynasty of Jeroboam was thus brought to an early end when all of the members of Jeroboam's family were murdered by the usurper's orders.

Baasha was vigorous, active, and dynamic. He was soon at war with Asa of Judah. In order to save his own land, it seemed necessary for Asa to call in Benhadad of Syria to attack Baasha. It was the beginning of a series of bitter struggles with the Syrians that so completely exhausted both countries that Assyria could run roughshod over them.

After twenty-four years of ruling, Baasha died, passing the responsibility to his drunken son Elah, who was promptly murdered by Zimri, one of his officers. It was easy to kill all the friends and relatives of Elah and to establish himself on the throne. After one whole week in the royal palace, the king was besieged by Omri and the rest of the army. When escape was cut off, Zimri committed suicide by burning the palace over his head. His victory had been short-lived.

Omri reigned for twelve years and did more for the

kingdom than any of his predecessors. His outstanding contribution was the building of the new capital city on the hill at Samaria. He thus established his throne on an impregnable hill where he could hope to defend himself against all enemies. It took the trained engineers of Assyria over two years to force their way into the fortress (in 722 B.C.).

Omri made an alliance with the Phoenicians by taking the Sidonian princess, Jezebel, for his son Ahab. It seemed to him a happy, diplomatic stroke, but it was destined to cause more trouble than any other move of the century. Jezebel came into the land with her Baal worship and thoroughly contaminated the people. She came definitely to change the religion of Israel from the simple worship of Jehovah to the worship of Baal and Astarte. Prophets of Jehovah were immediately silenced, and imported priests of the new religion took charge of the religious affairs of the land.

During Omri's day the Syrians were growing stronger and more cruel in their treatment of neighbors. Serious days were ahead for Israel as Damascus armed itself for the bitter struggle. For fifty years the people of the Northern Kingdom suffered from the cruel soldiers of the Syrians.

VII. AHAB AND JEZEBEL

Because we think of the powerful way that Jezebel managed her husband, we are prone to lose sight of the strength of the king. We are prejudiced against him, too, because of the rise of the heathen worship during his reign and the persecution of the loyal prophets. As a matter of fact, Ahab was a capable general, administrator, and king. As a successful warrior and progressive states-man, he built up the kingdom in a material way. His keen business sense was evident in his dealings with the neigh-boring people. He beautified and fortified his capital and built fine palaces and temples for his wife and her reli-gion. His "ivory palace" was famous for a century.

Ahab and Jehoshaphat "buried the hatchet" and en-tered into friendly alliance that spelled happier days for the kingdom. Instead of wasting his strength in exhaust-ing wars, Ahab used it in building up trade routes, cities, good will, and good government. Wealth was accumu-lated. Indeed, if riches and material success could be counted as the goal of a nation, Ahab's reign could be counted an unqualified success. Fortunately, there were people in the land who realized that ideals were more im-portant than unlimited wealth. The old faith, the old standards of morality, the old religion, were all breaking down under the low, enervating, degrading life of the luxury-minded people of the land. The base religions from Phoenicia and Canaan were leaving their impres-sion. Jehovah was being forgotten.

Jezebel was guilty of introducing another god to the people of Israel. They had been a people kept apart from such base influences as the introduction of Baal worship would necessarily bring. They were not prepared for the system of morals that they were called upon to face. The wicked queen forced the unwilling subjects to re-nounce their allegiance to Jehovah and become loyal to Baal. If prophets continued to preach, they were si-lenced. Regular Baal worship was set up and supported.

Jezebel's character came out clearly in her treatment of Naboth when he refused to sell his vineyard to Ahab.

She was unscrupulous enough to demand the murder of the owner of the property so that her husband might have it. It was an easy matter to kill this pious landowner and take the property for the king. Jezebel seemed to enjoy such use of power. She was not at all worried over the wrong perpetrated. The death of an innocent man meant nothing to her. She had won her point and was satisfied.

It was a dark day for Israel when Jezebel came into the royal palace. We have reason to believe that Ahab might have been a good ruler, had Jezebel not been his evil genius. He was forced to follow her lead and commit acts of oppression that were unthinkable. He knew that Solomon had brought in women of all the surrounding nations and had allowed each to introduce her own religion. Ahab wanted to be friendly to Phoenicia, and he realized that he had to allow Jezebel to do as she pleased. It would take the thundering voice of a great prophet of God to break down the rapid trend toward Baalism. God was preparing a prophet to stand in the breach and save the day for Jehovah religion. The crisis must be met. God was equal to the emergency and in his own good time brought forth his servant to strike a death blow at Baal worship. Elijah was God's man for the critical moment.

Loyalty to Baal and Jehovah could not exist side by side in the same land, because the controlling spirit of each was irrevocably hostile to the other. The Baal was sensual, immoral, autocratic, and lacking in all that was so necessary in the master of a soul. Jehovah was moral, spiritual, and a jealous God who would tolerate no rival in the affections of his people. The mission of Elijah was to convince the people of Jehovah's right to their best love and to cause them to choose him. It was a day of decision. The challenge was thrown out to them. How would they respond?

FOR CLASS DISCUSSION AND FURTHER STUDY

1. In what ways did Jeroboam I sow the seeds which were ultimately to bring about the destruction of his nation some two hundred years later? Using a complete concordance, see how many times you can find Jeroboam referred to as the one "who made Israel to sin," (or similar words).
2. Why is Rehoboam classed as "a weak ruler"?
3. Study the chart on page 55, noting the names of the rulers of Israel and Judah. As you read the accounts in 1 Kings 12–16 and 2 Chronicles 10–12, check the names of the godly kings. Does this study suggest one reason why the kingdom of Judah survived longer than did Israel?

CHAPTER 3

3

ELIJAH AND ELISHA

1 Kings 17–22; 2 Kings 1–9

JEZEBEL'S WICKED INFLUENCE soon permeated the land. But the dark picture was to form the background in which the work of the prophets developed.

I. A DISTRESSING SITUATION

The land of Israel faced a crisis. It had no preacher. Jezebel ruled with an iron hand and was quietly crushing out any lingering loyalty to Jehovah. The few remaining worshipers of the true God were afraid to show themselves. Ahab was not concerned with the struggle, since it did not make much difference to him which god they worshiped. He would have voted for Jehovah, but it would not have hurt him to see Baal win the election. The people were convinced that Baal was the one who gave them rain, crops, luxury, and good times.

II. ELIJAH

Although the people were practically ready to go over bodily to the camp of Baal, God was not willing to surrender. Elijah was his answer. Through the bold prophet Jehovah would bring his answer to the people.

1. *A Startling Announcement*

As Jezebel, Ahab, and the luxury-loving crowd were lounging in their comfortable palace, they were rudely startled by a crude, rough mountaineer who swooped down upon them with a mysterious pronouncement. God had answered the challenge of Baal by sending one of the most imposing figures of the age. Before that personality kings, courtiers, generals, and statesmen pale into insignificance. Elijah was a physical, spiritual, moral giant who strode into the midst of high society with the courage of his convictions and defied conventions, traditions, kings, and even the wicked Jezebel as he delivered his Master's burning message. The prophet's appearance, his garb, his sincerity, his flaming earnestness, and his power as a messenger threw consternation into the gathering. "As Jehovah, the God of Israel, liveth, before whom I stand, there shall not be dew nor rain these years, but according to my word" (1 Kings 17:1 ASV). What a message that was! Each word weighed a ton.

What did Elijah mean? Could he hope to have in his possession the keys to the heavens? How could he control the rain and the dew? He had been praying that a real test might be given so that all the people might know that Baal was not the giver of rain, dew, crops, and fertility. (See James 5:17–18.) They must realize that a serious drought could come in spite of all of Baal's efforts to supply water. It was a bold prediction, but the preacher had God's word for it and was certain that it could be sustained. Not a drop of moisture would come to the thirsty earth until the word was spoken by Elijah. Months would pass, and each day would only add to the mysterious solemnity of the word of the fearless prophet from Gilead. They were to face starvation, destitution, and death in order that Jehovah's power might be revealed.

2. *By the Brook Cherith*

Before the dumfounded group could seize the prophet, he was away. Without leaving a trace, Elijah concealed himself by a friendly brook, probably on the east side of the Jordan. There would be plenty of time before Ahab and his people understood all the message and learned its lessons. At any rate, the prophet could be certain of protection from Ahab and food to sustain life. He was under orders and had faith to believe in Jehovah's power and love. He knew that God would honor and care for his faithful servant.

Food was miraculously furnished, but Elijah was dependent upon the brook for his water supply. It was a real test of faith when he watched the steady decrease in the water. God was keeping his word in withholding rain from the earth, and Elijah's own drinking water was gradually giving out. What would he do when the waters ceased? How could he live without water? The prophet must have learned much from those days of watchful waiting. God became even more real to him as he became more dependent upon the Lord. Solitude helps us, but solitude brightened by the presence of God works wonders in the building of character.

3. *At Zarephath*

Before suffering came to the loyal soldier, a new command came from his Lord. Elijah was ordered to move entirely across the land of Israel and live for a season at Zarephath. On this journey he would pass through Jezebel's territory and into the land of Phoenicia, from which that terrible queen came. In other words, he was to face danger and possible death on a journey that would end in a small city by the sea near Jezebel's old home.

Following Jehovah's leading, Elijah came to the home of a poor widow in Zarephath. When she did all within her power to help feed the stranger, she was miraculously blessed. Jehovah continued to care for his prophet and also for the one who had so graciously offered to help.

The long sojourn in that foreign home was a good discipline for God's man. The people of Israel were suffering from the worst drought of their time, but the loyal soldier of God was cared for, protected, and made ready for his future work. Elijah's faith was strengthened for the impending crisis.

The son of his hostess died and was restored to life under the inspired touch of the servant of God. It was a signal victory that was allowed as a sure token of Jehovah's actual presence and power. After that significant event, Elijah must have been strong enough for any further word of command. His God was sufficient.

4. Meeting with Ahab

It took a great deal of courage to obey the divine voice and go out to meet the king of Israel. For three years that king had done his best to find the rough old preacher who had caused so much trouble. During all these years the ground had become harder and more desolate. The crops had failed. The horses and mules were dying. An entire nation was suffering, and the king was mad with rage. It was preposterous to think that a mere man should cause so much trouble in Israel.

With characteristic courage the prophet strode forth to find the king. Obadiah, a faithful steward of the king, was the first to meet Elijah. During the prophet's absence Obadiah had been saving the lives of many scores of loyal preachers.

When Ahab was called he came with much noise and clatter. At last he had found the man whom he wanted to punish! Such a man needed severe punishment. Had not he been a disturber of the entire people? Had he not caused a whole nation to suffer? The angry king found his match in the rugged man of God. Instead of heaping punishment upon the offender, the king felt the severe whip fall upon himself. Elijah was more than a match for Ahab. He charged all the suffering of the people to the wickedness of the king and his family.

Elijah gave a sharp command to the king: "Send, and gather to me all Israel unto mount Carmel, and the prophets of Baal four hundred and fifty, . . . which eat at Jezebel's table" (1 Kings 18:19).

What could a mere king do when confronted by one who held the keys to the heavens? How could he deny the request of the one who had caused his land to suffer for three years? The time had come for a convincing test. The people were hungry and thirsty and humbled. It was God's time to drive home a never-to-be-forgotten lesson.

5. *The Contest on Mount Carmel*

Ahab did his duty, and the people came to the top of Carmel in great numbers. The prophets of Baal were there, even though Jezebel did not accompany them. The multitude stood ready to hear the famous man and to render a decision on the basis of the facts presented in the test. Having suffered enough, they were ready to listen to reason.

Elijah took charge of the meeting immediately, throwing down a challenge to every listener to make up his mind and come out boldly for Jehovah or Baal. He promised a fair contest that would make clear to every rational mind who was the true God to worship. Let them watch closely, think clearly, and choose wisely.

Elijah then threw out his invitation to the prophets of Baal. Let them call upon their god and let him send fire in answer to their requests. Let them convince the people by showing what their god could do under pressure.

An altar was built, an offering placed upon it, and the prophets of Baal were invited to call on their god for proof. From morning until noon the prophets worked and called frantically. Baal did not answer. Elijah taunted them with ironical remarks: "Cry aloud; for he is a god: either he is musing, or he is gone aside, or he is on a journey, or peradventure he sleepeth and must be awaked" (1 Kings 18:27 ASV). This drove the dervishes to even wilder demonstrations. They leaped and danced and cut themselves until the blood spurted from many open wounds.

When they had failed, Elijah prepared for the big demonstration. The old altar to Jehovah was repaired, a trench was made around it, the bullock was laid on the wood, and plenty of water was poured over the entire altar. The true prophet knew his God and knew that he was going to answer.

Elijah prayed: "Hear me, O Jehovah, hear me, that this people may know that thou, Jehovah, art God" (1 Kings 18:37 ASV).

The answer came in a flash of lightning consuming the offering and the sacrifice. The people shouted, "Jehovah, he is God; Jehovah, he is God" (1 Kings 18:39 ASV). It was a glorious victory for Elijah and for the Eternal One. Surely there could not be any further question!

6. Prayer Answered

After promising Ahab that the three years' drought was about to be broken, Elijah went into a quiet place on Carmel to plead with Jehovah for the promised rain. His servant was sent to look out over the sea for evidences of rain, but continued to return to his master with the same discouraging report. In the face of such reports, and while looking upon a sky that looked like brass, the preacher continued to pray for rain. Finally, such prevailing faith won the victory. A cloud the size of a hand was seen over the sea. It was enough. Rain was coming! God had heard and answered! His name was honored among men. How could anyone doubt any longer?

Baal had been revealed as impotent in the land that had turned to him and also in the very element in which he had been thought the strongest. Jehovah had really demonstrated his right to the undivided allegiance of the nation. But it takes more than a rainstorm to break up a nation's bad habits. Elijah was to learn in a tragic manner that the victory was far from won. Temporary defeat was lurking just around the corner to trip the elated messenger of Jehovah, and it overtook him hard on the heels of his spectacular triumph.

7. *Running from Jezebel*

In the strength of these victories, Elijah plunged down the mountainside for twenty-two miles to receive the plaudits of the multitudes. Even Ahab's chariot was too slow for him. Surely Jezebel and her husband would now bow to him and honor him publicly! Certainly there could be no question of any remaining loyalty to Baal! His prophets were all dead and his cause dishonored. At the palace gate the elated prophet waited for the thrilling invitation.

Jezebel had no notion of surrender. She realized that Elijah had captured the popular fancy and that it would not be wise to punish him openly. She decided to scare him so much that he would run completely away and leave the field open for Baal's recuperation. Her threat was sufficient, and Elijah started on his long three-hundred-mile journey. It was more than one hundred miles to Beersheba, where he left his servant, and then at least two hundred miles farther to Horeb where he received his new commission.

Why did Elijah run away? Surely he had seen too many demonstrations of Jehovah's power and presence to fear a mere woman! For once the prophet seemed to get away without seeking guidance. He was tired, and he relaxed. Like most enthusiasts he had reacted to the other extreme. He was completely discouraged, and in this state it was easy to be frightened. The murderous message came at exactly the right moment to cause Elijah to lose what little courage and good sense he had. He had no reserves left to put into action except some physical strength that came to him in the crisis and caused his tired legs to respond. Southward from Jezreel and onward through the land of Judah he fled, thinking only of escape from a wicked queen. We cannot see how he covered the distance of one hundred miles to Beersheba, but when fear holds the reins, human strength often can do more than seems possible. The old prophet's servant fell by the way at Beersheba, but he himself did not dare stop until he had plunged farther into the wilderness.

8. God's Gracious Care

The same God who had provided food and water at Cherith and Zarephath was waiting at the juniper tree as his exhausted preacher collapsed. The same God who had given him the victory on Carmel was now ready to nourish and sustain his servant who had run away from Israel, but who had not drifted beyond Jehovah's love and tender care.

Elijah was so thoroughly exhausted and depressed that he did not care to live. Suicide was in his mind. After all, why should he live, since Jezebel had full power to thwart every move? In his depression he lost sight of the fact that Jehovah was more powerful than Jezebel.

Jehovah gave plenty of refreshing sleep as his first contribution to the poor fellow. After the rest he was awakened by the call to breakfast. A divinely prepared meal was necessary before reason could be found. When Elijah became a bit more rational, it was easy for God to lead him to understand that he was to go on into the wilderness, even to Mount Horeb (Sinai). Greater and richer revelations would be given to him in the quiet place of the sacred mount.

9. *God's Revelation at Horeb*

In the sacred atmosphere of Sinai, where the law had been given to Moses, it was possible for the prophet to find not only physical satisfaction but a spiritual experience that transformed his whole life. God allowed him to open his lips and tell all that had been heavy on his heart. All the complaints, doubts, discouragements, failures, and disappointments were poured out. Then the stormy wind, the terrifying earthquake, and the fire came to still his heart and turn his thoughts from himself to the might and majesty of the Eternal One. He knew that only God could do the things that had just been done. Reverently he waited for the divine manifestation.

As Elijah paused in the quiet aftermath, the air seemed radiant with God's blessed sunlight. The wind, the quaking, and the fire had gone. God was there. The "still small voice" brought its message to Elijah. He was stilled by the mysterious "steppings of Jehovah," and at last seemed willing to obey the divine call.

10. *The New Commission*

The call came to Elijah to go back to Jezebel's land to do some specific work for Jehovah. He was to anoint Hazael to be king of Syria, Jehu to be king of Israel, and Elisha to be a prophet to carry on his work after him. It was a great experience to realize that God really needed him and was planning to use him again. Jezebel would not be able to harm him if he were on a mission for Jehovah. It was a task that might stagger a young man, but the old veteran rallied under the call and prepared to do God's will.

Thus, God, by his wise dealing with his preacher, saved him from despondency, grief, fear, and a desire for death. Jehovah solved the problem by revealing himself to Elijah and then challenging him with a mighty call to definite work. Elijah marched away from Sinai with a new spring in his step, a new joy in his heart, a new light in his eyes, and a new work to do for his Lord.

11. *At Naboth's Vineyard*

It was a different man who met Ahab as he inspected his new vineyard. With all of the fire and courage of the great reformer that he was, Elijah attacked the king for his wickedness and injustice. He poured into the ear of Ahab the burning charge of Jehovah. The prediction of disgrace and death for the whole family was delivered to the shrinking man. We admire the preacher who so fearlessly spoke to the king. He definitely linked religion with social justice. The ethical and democratic nature of Jehovah's religion was put before Ahab and all peoples. The king repented and prayed for forgiveness with such genuineness that the sentence was delayed for a number of years. Elijah had "come back" with such a tremendous pressure that we are made to rejoice as we listen to the voice of the courageous prophet.

III. ELISHA

In the purpose of God, a successor of Elijah was raised up in the person of the gentle Elisha.

1. *The Call of Elisha*

One of God's definite commands to Elijah was to find and call the young man named Elisha. It must have been a joy for the older man to find and throw his mantle over the plowboy and to look forward to the days when the two should walk together as God's prophets. The young man was in the field with twelve teams of oxen under his supervision. Elisha understood fully the significance of the strange behavior of Elijah and went immediately into the work. For months, and possibly years, the youthful Elisha walked with and ministered to the older prophet. It was a great opportunity for him to learn at the feet of a noble teacher the hidden things of the kingdom of God.

As the two worked together during these years, much thought and effort were given to the organization and development of the theological schools for the training of future leaders. It was a significant movement in the land. God was richly blessing these two servants of his.

2. *Elijah Taken Home*

After a long life of usefulness the time came for the old preacher to go home. His young follower kept very close to him as they visited the bands of prophets at Bethel and Jericho. Crossing the Jordan, they made their way to the hills of Moab near the spot where Moses had been taken. Suddenly and without warning the chariot came and the master was borne away to rest with his God. His mantle fell upon the young prophet and the Spirit of God led him back to take up the work of preaching, teaching, and building for God. Jehovah's fiery champion was gone from the earth, but the plans of God were to be carried on by the gentle, kind, constructive builder who took up where Elijah left off and built wisely for his Lord.

3. Elisha Leads On

Elisha became the respected friend and adviser of kings. He was given the task of making effective in the political and social life of Israel the fundamental principles put forth by Elijah. He practically completed the elimination of all forms of Baal worship from the land.

He became the wonder-worker of Israel. God gave him miraculous power that he might do acts of mercy for many helpless and needy people. His healing of the great Naaman stands out as his most notable miracle.

By anointing Jehu king of Israel, Elisha carried out Jehovah's orders to Elijah, and put into office the one who exterminated the remaining members of the house of Ahab. Jezebel and all of her tribe were put to death.

Jehovah used these two prophets through many years to put down Baal worship and evil practices and to enthrone his blessed name in the land as the only God. Our hats are off to Elijah and Elisha!

FOR CLASS DISCUSSION AND FURTHER STUDY

1. What does the experience of Ahab demonstrate about the dangers of marriage with one who holds different religious beliefs?
2. What results were achieved in Israel through the ministry of Elijah? Compare the temperaments of Elijah and Elisha. Compare their achievements.

CHAPTER 4

4

A CENTURY OF TURMOIL

2 Kings 9–14; 2 Chronicles 22–26

IN THE YEAR 842 B.C., new rulers came to the thrones of
Syria, of Israel, and of Judah respectively. Jehu killed the
king of Judah and the king of Israel, while Hazael
smothered the king of Syria. Athaliah, the daughter of
Jezebel, took over the government in Judah. Jehu reigned
in Israel, and Hazael in Syria.

I. THE REVOLT UNDER JEHU

God had predicted that the house of Ahab must fall.
A young soldier, Jehu, heard the prophet Elijah tell Ahab
about the calamity that was to come. Years passed and
Ahab's son came to the throne for two years. He in turn
was followed by Jehoram for twelve years. Elisha knew
that Jehovah was tired of the house of Ahab and had left
orders for Jehu to be anointed king.

1. *Jehu Anointed*

To carry out the divine will, Elisha sent a young theological student to anoint Jehu and start him out in his
work as king. Jehu and his followers were elated over the
developments and rode off rapidly to finish the work.

Ahaziah, the king of Judah, was in Israel visiting his cousin Jehoram, the king of Israel.

2. *Retribution on the House of Ahab*

When Jehu rode into town, it was an easy matter for him to put both kings to death. He had himself proclaimed king in the North and set out immediately to exterminate all the house of Ahab. Jezebel was one of his first victims. Jehu seemed to take peculiar delight in driving his chariot over the broken form of the haughty queen. She had caused enough trouble, bringing calamity upon her family, upon the nation, and ultimately upon herself. Divine retribution had come.

The two kings had been shot on the very spot where Elijah had delivered his message concerning God's displeasure because of the treatment of Naboth. The dogs licked the blood and ate the flesh of Jezebel. Every one of the descendants of Ahab who was left in the land was cruelly slain. Jehu was leaving no stone unturned. He was to rule as an Oriental despot. He excused some of his cruel acts by claiming that he was merely carrying out the definite prophecy of Elijah and doing God's will in bringing destruction to the house of Ahab.

3. *Followers of Baal Massacred*

The mighty work of driving Baal from the land was begun by Elijah and continued by Elisha. It remained for Jehu to put on the finishing touches. He made up his mind that he would uproot every vestige of Baalism from the land. By a clever strategem he gathered every follower of Baal into the temple erected to Baal for a great sacrifice. From all over the land they came to join in the great meeting. All followers of Jehovah were expelled from the room, and then the slaughter began. Eighty armed executioners did their bloody work so thoroughly that not a man escaped. The temple and all of its furniture were burned and the place cursed. It was a bloody massacre, but it was Jehu's way of doing the thing. The Baal worshipers were disloyal to Jehovah and therefore traitors to the state. At any rate, the land was never bothered by Baal again.

4. Days of Trouble for Jehu

Even though Jehu had started out with such a reckless display of power and courage, he came during his later days to feel the cruel hand of the invaders. The great king of Assyria (Shalmanezer) came up from the far northeast with a mighty army against the peoples of Palestine. Jehu had murdered practically all the young leaders and was not able to put a creditable army in the field to aid Hazael of Syria in his efforts to repel the Assyrian invasion. In order to save his land, Jehu decided to buy off the invader with gold, silver, and precious gifts. It was a tragic moment when Israel began to buy her freedom from enemies. It meant that she would have to continue it all through the years. It was an open confession of weakness before the whole world.

Hazael was exceedingly bitter towards Jehu as a result of his actions. When Shalmanezer had gone back to Assyria, Hazael began seeking revenge. Israel was punished severely by the fine army of Syria. Cities were burned, young men slaughtered, women butchered, and babies crushed before parents' eyes. All the land of Israel on the east side of the Jordan River was lost. The bitter struggle continued all the days of Jehu and for practically thirty years following his death.

5. An Evaluation of Jehu

Jehu was a strong, resolute, rough, unscrupulous man whom Jehovah used in one of the most strategic periods of Israel's history. His reign was bathed in blood and strewn with wreckage all the way. His latter days were unhappy ones because of the serious opposition of enemies and because of the loss of prestige and the decline in prosperity among his own people. His work was significant. His character was not without serious blot. He will not allow us to forget him.

II. THE WICKED ATHALIAH

Athaliah, Jezebel's daughter, was queen in Judah during the reign of her husband Jehoram, and queen mother during the reign of her son Ahaziah. She had come to Jerusalem to live when the alliance had been perfected by Jehoshaphat and Ahab. She inherited her mother's strength of will and gave evidence of a fanatical zeal for Baal worship. Being much stronger than her husband, Athaliah easily forced him to murder six of his brothers and several of the other princes of the realm.

When her husband died the wicked queen was still the dominant force in the kingdom, while her son Ahaziah sat on the throne. That reign lasted only one year, for Jehu put an end to the career of Ahaziah.

Athaliah was so fanatical, wicked, and unscrupulous that she was willing to resort to a bloody massacre in order to satisfy her thirst for power. She was willing to murder her own grandsons. When the blood was cleaned away, she took her place on the throne, not knowing that the baby boy (Jehoash) had been kept alive by his aunt Jehosheba, the wife of the priest. For six years he had been kept safely in the Temple in the private apartment of Jehoiada, while the wicked woman ruled in Jerusalem. Athaliah must have been a woman of extraordinary genius to have occupied the throne of David for these years.

Baal worship was being crushed to death in Israel, but it was thriving in Jerusalem. Jezebel and her followers were put to death by Jehu, but Athaliah was giving Baal a stronghold in David's capital. The Temple of Jehovah was not only neglected but seems to have been partially wrecked to provide material for a temple to Baal.

Jehoiada and Jehosheba were in full charge of the Temple, and evidently Athaliah did not visit them in their apartment. While the boy, Jehoash, was growing the priest was laying his plans for the overthrow of the usurper. The people were tiring of Athaliah and were ready for the relief that was promised. The plot was carefully laid and the execution was perfect.

The boy (Jehoash) was introduced to the soldiers and crowned as the new king in David's dynasty. The people were wild in their acclaim of the boy king. Athaliah heard the shouting and came to investigate, only to meet the death that she so richly deserved. Thus came to an end the career of one of the worst characters that Jerusalem had known.

III. JEHOASH (JOASH) AND HIS REFORMS

It is well to remember that the young king was a grandson of Athaliah and Jehoram. How could he hope to be worth anything in the world? When all the other grandsons were slain, the infant was kept safely in the Temple of God. Those who guarded his life knew the one place in the city that would not be visited by the usurper. It was during those formative years that the boy was under the tutelage of the good old priest, Jehoiada. Too much credit cannot be given to that pious old couple, Jehoiada and Jehosheba, who saved the boy and brought him up in God's house.

After Jehoash's coronation he was still a child, and he needed the guidance of a strong hand. Jehoiada was the ruler during those early years, and began instigating some necessary reforms. We may be sure that it was quite a task to rid the city of the guards and officials who had been instruments of Athaliah. The city government was as corrupt as it is possible to imagine.

As the youngster grew into manhood, he showed evidences of his fine religious training. He leaned heavily upon the wisdom of the priest and tried to do God's will. King Jehoash was especially interested in the Temple and sought to prepare it for worship again after all the abuses it had suffered.

Jehoash called for contributions and requested the priests to assume responsibility for the collection of the money and for the repairing of the building. After a number of years had passed, he found that the priests had been using all the money for themselves and that the Temple was not being repaired.

Jehoash devised the plan of a box with a hole bored in its lid and placed where all good givers might deposit their contributions. At stated intervals the box was to be opened by two appointed officials who should use the

money as directed by the king. The expedient proved
brilliantly successful. The money poured in. The repairs
were made, and the people were again happy in the worship of Jehovah. They had plenty of money in the treasury for the purchase of new vessels to replace the ones
taken away in former days.

As long as the good old priest lived, all went well, and
Jehoash ruled wisely. He gave much attention to the
purification of the worship and the destruction of idols.
When Jehoiada died, a sudden change was manifest. The
wicked princes came to the king demanding a change
which would allow idolatry, heathen rites and altars, and
a lowering of existing standards of morality. Jehoash was
weak enough to allow them to have their way. Soon the
heathen party was ruling again. Zechariah, the high
priest who succeeded his father, Jehoiada, to the office,
came out boldly against the new deal, but he was unable
to stem the tide that was running out.

Jehoash ordered the execution of the priest for his
opposition to the new order. Such ingratitude and folly
has seldom been seen among men. Surely the king could
have been more kind to the son of his benefactor and
friend! It was an act that could never be explained.
Zechariah's dying words were, "Jehovah look upon it, and
require it" (2 Chron. 24:22 ASV). Such a blot should
never have been brought upon the name of the one who
was saved from death and brought up to be a king in
Jerusalem.

The closing years of the life of Jehoash were filled with
troubles and miseries. Hazael of Damascus came with a
strong army and subdued all the land of Palestine except
Jerusalem. In order to save his city, Jehoash collected

every available piece of gold and silver and sent it to the greedy Syrian. He withdrew from the land, but left the kingdom in bad condition.

The king's failure in his religious program and in the affairs of state caused a great wave of hatred to sweep the country. Feeling against him ran high. Even his physical sufferings failed to win sympathy for him, and he was brutally assassinated by his own officers as he slept in the stronghold at Millo. They took his body to Jerusalem, but he was not given a place in the royal sepulchers.

IV. THE PROPHET JOEL

It is probable that Joel came to preach to the people of Jerusalem during the early days of king Jehoash. The land was suffering severely from the worst drought and the worst locust plague that any of them had ever remembered. It was a serious time when priests, husbandmen, drunkards, and even the beasts of burden were joining their piteous cries of distress and thirst. Death was lurking just around the corner for all of them unless relief came.

Joel had a remedy to suggest. Let every man, woman, and child come together in a solemn assembly to seek God's will and to repent of their sins. It was a genuine call to repentance. Nothing short of that would satisfy Jehovah. Sin had held sway long enough. God was thoroughly disgusted with his people and had brought these afflictions upon them. "Yet even now, saith Jehovah, turn ye unto me with all your heart, and with fasting, and with weeping, and with mourning: and rend your heart, and not your garments, and turn unto Jehovah your God; for he is gracious and merciful, slow to anger, and abundant in lovingkindness, and repenteth him of the evil" (Joel 2:12–13 ASV).

Between Joel 2:17 and 2:18 we must suppose a scene in which Jehovah heard the prayers of the prophet and his people, and we are told of the fine blessings which were promised to repentant suppliants. Material and spiritual blessings were promised in abundance. The locusts would die and the rains would come to guarantee abundant vegetation. The Spirit of God was to be poured out in rich measure upon all the people. Not only at Pentecost was this blessed promise fulfilled.

Joel's message bore fruit and caused the people to turn to their God with a genuine prayer for help. God heard and answered. We are indebted to Joel for his challenging call. We need his message in our own day. What a blessing it would be if God's people who are called by his name would humble themselves and pray and seek his face and turn away from their wicked ways! (2 Chron. 7:14). They could expect all the rich blessings which were promised by Joel.

V. Two Great Monarchs

Following the death of Jehoash of Judah, the throne was in the hands of Amaziah, his son. He was a very foolish young man, who won a victory over the Edomites and brought the conquered idols back to be set up as his gods. Being puffed up with pride, Amaziah challenged the king of Israel to a battle, only to suffer a very humiliating defeat and to lose all of his valuables that were worth taking away. His own people turned against him, and he was killed.

Uzziah in Judah and Jeroboam II in Israel reigned side by side for nearly a half century. It was a period of prosperity, luxury, and plenty. Neighboring nations were weak and were soon paying tribute to these kings. Syria had given endless trouble for fifty years, but had now lost her hold in the West. We shall do well to study the fine work of these two monarchs who meant so much to the two kingdoms during the eighth century. They were able during their reigns to restore the territories of Israel and Judah to the area reached under David and Solomon. It was an era of unprecedented tranquillity and prosperity. Every sign pointed to a long-continued age of happiness and peace.

1. *Uzziah*

Uzziah reigned in Jerusalem for forty years and spent his time driving back enemies, capturing outposts (including the important seaport), building walls, cities, vineyards, aqueducts, and doing much to improve the living conditions of his people. In every phase of the work he was exceptionally helpful. Wealth began to pour into his land, and a strong class of nobles began to grow powerful. As wealth accumulated, religion came to have a harder time. Men forgot God when they became independent.

2. *Jeroboam II*

Jeroboam II reigned in Samaria for about forty years and performed in much the same way that his Judean contemporary did. He was a great warrior and was able in a short while to extend the boundaries to their farthest limit. The power of Damascus was broken. Edom, Moab, and Ammon were once more in the hands of the Israelites. Prosperity came in with the returning tides of trade. Palaces and public buildings were built and furnished lavishly for the pleasure-mad people.

VI. AN UNWILLING MISSIONARY

Jonah preached during the days of Jeroboam II (2 Kings 14:25) and predicted the unrivaled prosperity of the king. When God disturbed Jonah by a call to go to Nineveh, the capital of Assyria, with a message of doom, he was unwilling to go. His work was all that he wanted. He did not want to be a foreign missionary. He hated the Assyrians and did not want to see them spared. They were bitter enemies and nothing could please him better than news of their destruction.

When Jonah sought freedom by fleeing toward the west he was caught, convicted, punished, and miraculously preserved by a loving God who does not like disobedience. He learned that it was not so easy to refuse to do God's will. He learned, too, that God's power was absolute.

It was much easier for Jonah to go to Nineveh to carry God's ultimatum after the submarine journey. The message that he preached had an electric effect upon the people of that heathen city. They repented and complied fully with the divine requirement. Jonah was sorely displeased because God did not carry out his announced purpose to destroy the Assyrians. His narrow, selfish disposition showed itself in his ugly conduct. God had to teach him a missionary lesson by revealing his love for all men everywhere. The fact that they were of another nation did not cause God to cease loving them. God was only too glad to spare and care for them.

God cared enough for a heathen city to send one of his greatest preachers to preach to them. He accepted their repentance just as he accepted the cry of his own Chosen People. Surely we may catch a glimpse of Jehovah's love for the people of China, Japan, India, Africa, and the other countries of the world! May we be brought to love them as he loves, and do our part in the work of warning and wooing the peoples of the earth. The same God expects obedience from us and will honor our witnessing and save those who will repent and believe upon him.

FOR CLASS DISCUSSION AND FURTHER STUDY

1. As you consider the work of Jehu, enumerate his strong points; list his wicked or weak acts. Why did God use such a man in carrying out the divine purpose?
2. Evaluate the character and achievements of Jehoash. Why did he not continue in his strong stand for Jehovah?
3. In what sense is it true that God brings drought and other disasters on a land?

CHART OF OLD TESTAMENT HISTORY *

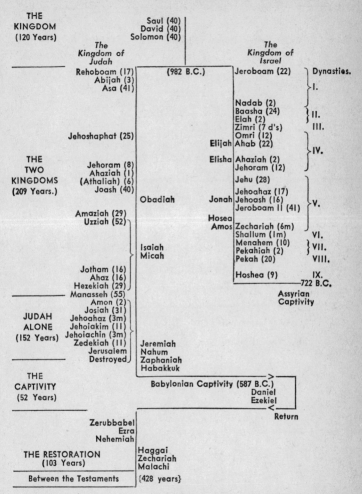

THE KINGDOM (120 Years)	Saul (40) David (40) Solomon (40)	

The Kingdom of Judah　　　　　　*The Kingdom of Israel*

THE KINGDOM (120 Years)	Saul (40) David (40) Solomon (40)	
	The Kingdom of Judah	*The Kingdom of Israel*
	Rehoboam (17) (982 B.C.) Jeroboam (22)	Dynasties.
	Abijah (3)	I.
	Asa (41)	
		Nadab (2)
		Baasha (24) } II.
		Elah (2)
		Zimri (7 d's) III.
	Jehoshaphat (25)	Omri (12)
	Elijah Ahab (22)	IV.
THE TWO KINGDOMS (209 Years.)	Elisha Ahaziah (2) Jehoram (12)	
	Jehoram (8)	Jehu (28)
	Ahaziah (1)	Jehoahaz (17)
	(Athaliah) (6)	Jonah Jehoash (16) V.
	Joash (40) Obadiah	Jeroboam II (41)
	Amaziah (29) Hosea	
	Uzziah (52) Amos	Zechariah (6m)
		Shallum (1m) VI.
	Isaiah	Menahem (10) } VII.
	Micah	Pekahiah (2) VIII.
		Pekah (20)
	Jotham (16)	Hoshea (9) IX.
	Ahaz (16)	722 B.C.
	Hezekiah (29)	Assyrian Captivity
	Manasseh (55)	
JUDAH ALONE (152 Years)	Amon (2) Josiah (31) Jehoahaz (3m) Jehoiakim (11) Jehoiachin (3m) Zedekiah (11) Jerusalem Destroyed	
	Jeremiah Nahum Zaphaniah Habakkuk	
THE CAPTIVITY (52 Years)	Babylonian Captivity (587 B.C.) Daniel Ezekiel	
		Return
THE RESTORATION (103 Years)	Zerubbabel Ezra Nehemiah Haggai Zechariah Malachi	
Between the Testaments	{428 years}	

* Adapted from chart by P. E. Burroughs in *Outlines of Bible History*. Because not all Bible chronology can be fixed exactly, there is some variation in dates in this chart and in the body of the text.

CHAPTER 5

5

AMOS AND HOSEA

Amos 1–9; Hosea 1–14

DURING THE DAYS of Jeroboam II and Uzziah there came upon the scene two of the most interesting characters of the whole era. These two prophets were called of God to preach to people who were growing richer and more worldly with every passing day. Kings, princes, priests, and people were all corrupt and needed a call from one of God's messengers to set them right again.

I. AMOS, THE HERDSMAN OF TEKOA (760 B.C.)

Amos grew up and labored in southern Judah about twelve miles south of Jerusalem. His work as a follower of sheep and a dresser of sycamore trees kept him in the open and also secluded from the outside world. We do not know how he was trained or how he came to know so much about the world situation.

1. *His Call*

Amos tells us that he was called from the field, and the hand of God was heavy upon him as he went to carry the message to sinners. He disclaimed membership in the prophetic guilds and claimed that he was a special envoy of Jehovah who had been drafted for definite serv-

ice. The bands of prophets were not in good standing
with the thinking people.

We may be sure that Amos' rough, meager fare, his
hard toil, his constant fight with cruel circumstances, and
his communion with God, helped to make him ready for
the crisis. He was a thorough student of world affairs.
Assyria, Egypt, Syria, Edom, Ammon, and Phoenicia
were known to him, and the hidden mysteries seemed to
be clear to him. History was an open book and the existing conditions of his day were not hidden from him. He
was a world citizen who could think clearly, speak courageously, and interpret God's will without fear. He had
graduated from God's university.

Amos' call into the service was the most important
event in his life. It was Jehovah's definite commission to
go under divine compulsion to the designated spot with
a definite message. God came upon him to give him new
powers of discernment and discrimination. Prediction
was possible for him as well as power of interpretation
and application. He was God's man.

2. *The Festival at Bethel*

Just twenty-two miles north of Tekoa was Bethel, the
principal open-air shrine of Israel. Jeroboam had set up
calf worship there in 931 B.C. When Amos was directed
to go on a special mission to Bethel, it was a big feast
day. Pilgrims were there from all parts of the land, with
their fine clothes, rich offerings, loud music, and festive
airs. The priests, dressed in the most colorful robes,
chanted weird melodies, while their assistants worked
feverishly to kill, prepare, and offer the innumerable
sacrifices. Altars reeked with the blood of bulls and goats.

Burning flesh left its peculiar aroma on every side. Everybody was bent on having a good time and offering the finest sacrifice possible. The people were exceedingly religious. The high priest was happy that they were having such a successful day.

3. *The Strange Intruder*

Into this happy, carefree, sinful group, the strange prophet from Tekoa walked. It seemed too bad that such a gathering had to be interrupted. When Amos began to speak, the people welcomed him as a novel sort of entertainer who would probably provide a bit of amusement for the crowd. They gathered around to listen. How could a preacher hope to make any impression on such a group of people? They were not in any mood to listen to rebuke and warning. How could the awkward country preacher grip their attention and hold them long enough to preach to them a needed message? Let us step back in time and watch him as he reveals his extraordinary power as a speaker. Let us watch the crowd as they are skilfully caught in his net and held while the chastisement is administered. Amos was an artist of the rarest sort.

4. *The Charge Against the Nations*

Amos began by turning his guns on Damascus. Jehovah was against Syria and would bring ruin upon her because of cruel acts of barbarism. In quick succession he turned upon the other neighbors—Philistia, Ammon, Moab, and Edom. Each was condemned for shameless acts of atrocity and impiety that violated every rule of war. For each of these offenders Jehovah was preparing a measure of doom that would fit the offense. We may

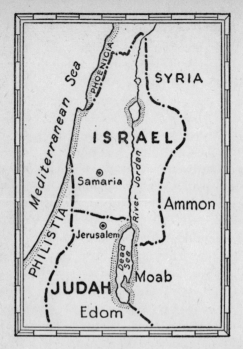

well imagine the shouts of approval that came from Amos' hearers as a result of this castigation of the neighbors. In each case the Israelites hated the enemy nation and would take peculiar delight in the sudden destruction of its capital city.

In addition to these enemy nations, Amos brought a specific charge against Judah and announced doom as the certain portion of that land. Judah had failed miserably in living up to the standard that had been set for her. In spite of prophets, laws, teachings, miraculous interventions, and divine blessings, Judah had continued in sin.

5. *The Sudden Turn upon Israel*

The master artist had a grip on his audience that could not be broken. They were ready to vote him the greatest preacher of the age, when suddenly he turned and confronted them with charges more serious and deadly than all the others combined. They could not move away. They simply stood and took his terrific broadside against them. They were even more guilty than their less enlightened neighbors. They must be held to a higher standard. They were God's elect nation. That election carried with it terrific responsibility and dread consequences.

The very people who were parading their piety were guilty of oppressing the poor, of drunkenness, injustice, covetousness, lasciviousness, sacrilege, usury, unchastity, enslavement of fellow Hebrews, and rejecting the messages of Jehovah. The courts were venal, the rich were rapacious, the women were heartless and selfish in their ungodly demands upon their men. Amos called the carousing women "kine [cows] of Bashan" (Amos 4:1). Debauchery, extortion, reckless waste, unbridled passions, heartless cruelty, unjust dealings, corrupt judges, and vile thoughts, all came under the swift blows of the inspired orator. Jehovah had stirred him to action. He could not refrain from speaking. The groans of the suffering masses fired him with a new fervor. The champion of justice was roaring forth God's message of doom.

6. *Certain Captivity Predicted*

Amos was able to see clearly the certain punishment that was ahead. Humanly speaking, God had reached the end of his patience. The idols, altars, ivory palaces, and the idle loafers were to perish together. The eternal God who had created and moved nations was about to manifest his power. Righteousness had reached its limit of endurance. The people could not expect to be spared in the face of such sins and failures. God was raising up a destroyer who would bring terrible punishment.

7. A Great Challenge

In the face of such dire calamity, the prophet was strangely moved. He could not see his people rushed away into exile without an effort to win them. His call to repentance and godly living was sincere, earnest, and powerful. He challenged them to be done with bribery, debauchery, injustice, false living, and turn to God with all their hearts. He wanted righteousness in public and private life. "Hate the evil, and love the good, and establish justice in the gate: it may be that Jehovah, the God of hosts, will be gracious unto the remnant of Joseph. But let justice roll down as waters, and righteousness as a mighty stream" (Amos 5:15,24 ASV). Such a call should have challenged the best in the hearts of the men of Israel. Amos could see, out of the ruins of the old state, a new state arising with the smile of Jehovah upon it. The fallen "tabernacle" of David (9:11) would be restored in all of its old glory.

8. Amos Opposed by Amaziah, the Priest

It was more than the hireling priest could stand. Amaziah must have been embarrassed beyond words for quite a while before he found an opportunity to speak. He resented the attacks from the rude intruder. There was too much truth in his words for comfort. Finally, Amos gave him an opening when he said that Jehovah would "rise against the house of Jeroboam with the sword" (Amos 7:9 ASV).

Amaziah sent a messenger to the king, denouncing Amos as a traitor. "Amos hath conspired against thee. . . . For thus Amos saith, Jeroboam shall die by the sword, and Israel shall surely be led away captive out of his land" (Amos 7:10–11 ASV).

Immediately Amaziah turned upon the preacher and ordered him to leave the country. With a sneer he accused Amos of being a member of one of the discredited groups of "prophets" who talked for money, saying in effect: "Off with you to Judah! Earn your bread there, and there play the prophet. But at Bethel you shall prophesy no more; for it is the king's sanctuary and the royal residence" (7:12–13). It was one of the most significant encounters of all religious history. The priestly champion of aristocratic privilege stood over against the one man of God who calmly demanded ethical and social reform.

Amos indignantly denied the charges of being a selfish prophet after easy money. He claimed to be Jehovah's special messenger to chastise such an hireling as Amaziah. It was a mighty indictment that he launched against the priest. It was necessary for Amos to leave Israel and go back to his native land. He had carried God's message faithfully and forcefully.

9. *Some Teachings of Amos*

The message of Amos contains certain timeless principles, which apply to our own day:

1. Amos taught very clearly that Jehovah was God of all the earth and not a mere tribal god as so many of the people seemed to think. He had absolute control in Palestine, Syria, Philistia, Ammon, Phoenicia, Edom, and Assyria. Nothing could cause him to fail in any venture he started. He was the sovereign Lord.

2. Amos emphasized the idea and practice of social righteousness. He demanded justice in dealing with one another. No amount of pious profession was worth anything when men were unwilling to be honest, just, clean, and righteous.

3. In his teaching, privilege involved responsibility. The Syrians, Philistines, and Phoenicians were held to a certain standard. The Israelites were measured by a much higher standard because they had been given so much greater privileges. They had been brought out of Egypt, given a new land, miraculously preserved, and prophets had come to them with divine directions. Were they not favorites of Jehovah? Surely he would not dare inflict punishment upon them! He says: "You only have I known of all the families of the earth: *therefore* [author's italics] I will visit upon you all your iniquities" (Amos 3:2 ASV). The hand of God would be heavy upon them.

4. The prophet's emphasis upon the right sort of worship was one of his finest contributions. Mere formal worship was an abomination in God's eyes. The music, the ritual, the offerings, the prayers, were utterly distasteful to a holy God when they came from cold, sinful, corrupt, unchastened hearts. Jehovah turned away in disgust from such performances. "Let justice roll down as waters, and righteousness as a mighty stream" (Amos 5:24 ASV).

II. Hosea, the Prophet of Love

The most prosperous days of Israel were enjoyed during the reign of Jeroboam II. Peace, plenty, luxury, ease, false standards, sin, and indulgence were the ruling marks of the age. Amos did his best to warn the people and their rulers and to point out for them the sure symptoms of ruin and disaster. They refused to be alarmed or to change their sinful course.

1. *The Times in Which Hosea Lived*

When Hosea came upon the scene a few years later he found anarchy, bloodshed, and ruin staring the nation in the face. "There is no truth, nor goodness, nor knowledge of God in the land. There is nought but swearing and breaking faith, and killing, and stealing, and committing adultery; they break out, and blood toucheth blood" (Hosea 4:1–2 ASV).

In the midst of such conditions, Jehovah sent his message by his shrinking young prophet. The cruel Assyrian was preparing his war chariots for the journey into the West. The kingdom of Israel was hastening toward its fall. God was the only hope. Hosea was thrust into the breach to stop the downward rush by urging them to return to God, who alone could save them.

2. *Hosea's Personal Problems*

The story opens with the picture of a young preacher and his bride building a home together. Hosea's love for Gomer was a love that transcends all pictures of love that literature has preserved for us—Robert Browning, Romeo, Leander, or any other.

Children came into the home, but it became increasingly clear to the young husband that his wife did not love him. She was playing around with other lovers who promised her more of the glitter of worldly living. He soon became certain that she was false to him. Unfaithfulness is an ugly word, but it is the word to use.

When Hosea came home to find that Gomer had gone out with other lovers, leaving the children to him, he might have dismissed the matter with a wave of his hand and been grateful for such a fortunate deliverance from one so base. Instead, he suffered untold agony as he poured out his heart in weeping. He truly loved her, and that love was stronger than death. He suffered alone as he continued to love one who was untrue.

3. A New Realization

As Hosea sobbed his heart out in the midnight darkness, he became conscious of another voice that was sobbing. It shocked him to learn that it was God's voice and that Jehovah was actually sobbing. He had never thought of God in that way. Why should he sob? What could cause God to suffer? Gradually it dawned upon him that God's people (his bride) had gone off in the hills of Canaan with other lovers (Baal and other false gods). Hosea caught a vision of Jehovah deserted, lonely, forsaken, heartbroken, and sad. God's great heart was torn and bleeding. His people had defiled themselves with the heathen gods. The old covenant had been broken by these faithless lovers. Instead of casting them off as vile sinners, unfit for his plan, God loved them, yearned for them, and sought earnestly to attract them to himself again. It was a picture of a God who was a true lover and whose love would never give up until the people came back.

4. A New Understanding of God

As the young prophet thought on the matter, he came to see God in a new light. As he came close to Jehovah, Hosea caught a new conception of sin. It was much more hideous and gruesome than he had ever imagined. It was the vilest, the blackest, the ugliest thing that he had ever known. He saw it as "cutting the optic nerve of the soul." Just as a certain disease may cut the optic nerve, making sight impossible, so has sin a way of deadening and killing the nerve that makes spiritual vision possible. The people who had sinned had come to the place where it was impossible to discern spiritual things. God's chosen ones had lost the power to appreciate and understand God and his love for them.

To the prophet, Jehovah came to be a real person who was alive, near, active, and capable of strong feeling. In fact, he was the lover-God whose love was unquenchable. Disappointment, sin, corrupt living, false professions only served to make God cling with more tenacity to his loved ones.

This was a new idea for the world. The people had thought of God as a being who enjoyed unlimited power, who chose to do as he pleased, enjoyed war and conquest, who ruled as a great monarch. Hosea learned through intimate touch with Jehovah to know him as a God of infinite tenderness who was definitely in love with all his sinning children.

5. *A New Challenge*

Through the long hours the heart of the young preacher continued to yearn for the one he loved. He hated her sin, but he loved her. He could not forget her. His heart was still broken, and in his hours of anguish he continued to dream of the day when she would be willing to come back to his home again.

As Hosea's heart cried out for the wife of his love, she was being sold into slavery. The lovers who had promised so much had already tired of her. Her life was miserable as she was kicked around from one owner to another.

One day the word of Jehovah came to Hosea asking him to go out into the city to find that sinning wife and bring her home again. She was not fit for his home. She certainly did not deserve such treatment.

It was a matter easily and quickly settled for this young lover. Instantly he made his way across the wicked city to bring Gomer home again. When he found her in the clutches of a slave dealer, he realized that she had lost the beauty and attractiveness that used to make her the pride of his eyes. The face was not beautiful, the eyes were unattractive, the years had exacted their toll, dissipation had been unkind to her. No one wanted to buy such a wreck as she had become.

The thrilling moment came when Hosea finally won Gomer's consent to come back to his home and his heart again. He went forward to the auction block and deposited the money and took her away from these evil companions to his own heart again. (He very probably complied with the requirements of the Mosaic law in leaving her in what we would call a hospital until she was well and clean and fit again.) It was love's beautiful triumph.

6. *The Wooing Note in Hosea's Preaching*

It was a new preacher who went out among the wandering people. Hosea had learned of the mighty love of God that never ceased until the loved one was brought back. He told his hearers that Jehovah still loved them and that he would not give them up until they returned. God promised them kindness, consideration, love, tenderness, and healing. "I will heal their backsliding, I will love them freely" (Hosea 14:4 ASV). They would be restored to the old place in God's heart and affection. Jehovah had been faithful, kind, and loving even though they had gone off after Baal and other false gods.

Hosea begged them to come back with tears and confessions. God would forgive and bless every one of them. With love, earnestness, and zeal the prophet appealed to sinning men to hearken to God and come home. He was an effective interpreter of God's great heart to men.

FOR CLASS DISCUSSION AND FURTHER STUDY

1. The author says: "Amos was an artist of the rarest sort." Do you agree with this statement? (1) Consider his approach. How did he win his audience? (2) How did he "apply" his message to his hearers? (3) To what extent did Amos become emotionally involved in the message?
2. Try to secure and read *Studies in Hosea* by K. Owen White. Discuss the designation "Hosea, prophet of love" and show why it is applicable.
3. In what way was the concept of God which Hosea presented new to his people?

CHAPTER 6

6

JUDAH'S GOLDEN AGE

2 Kings 15–20; 2 Chronicles 26–32;
Micah 1–7; Isaiah 1–66

THE EIGHTH CENTURY was a great era for prophecy. Amos and Hosea preached in the Northern Kingdom, while Isaiah and Micah delivered God's messages in Jerusalem. These four men rank among the leaders in that long line of speakers for God. They represented him to the people and sought to call men back to the standards that had been set for them. Amos and Hosea did their best with the men of Israel, who were rushing so rapidly toward captivity. It seems that their calls went unheeded, for there was no appreciable change in the conduct of the rebels. They were on the toboggan, and nothing could break the precipitous rush toward exile.

I. PRECEDING HISTORY

In 722 B.C., after a long siege, the city of Samaria was captured by the Assyrians under the leadership of Sargon II. The people were taken away to Nineveh, and the Northern Kingdom came to an end. Nineteen kings had sat on the throne from 931–722 B.C. Jeroboam's kingdom passed from the picture never to return.

In Judah, Uzziah builded wisely and well. He left to

his son Jotham a kingdom in the pink of condition. Ahaz followed Jotham and reigned for sixteen years. He was weak, hostile to the prophets, and uninterested in the continuance of Jehovah worship. Isaiah tried his best to lead the king to please God but to no avail. Ahaz' trouble with Pekah of Israel and Rezin of Syria was of such a serious nature that he called in the mighty Tiglath-pileser of Assyria to help him. This was a disastrous move, as Isaiah told him. Tiglath came with a great host of soldiers and practically ruined Syria and Israel. Ahaz was called on to pay homage to his new lord. It was a disastrous day for Judah when Tiglath took control.

II. Hezekiah, the Daring Young King

Hezekiah followed Ahaz on the throne of Judah, ruling for twenty-nine years. He was a better man than his father and did his best to lead the people back to God. He found that he had inherited from his father a shattered army, a ruined peasantry, an unprotected frontier, an empty treasury, a profaned temple, a lowered morale, and a godless people who had been led away from Jehovah by Ahaz. It was a serious task that confronted the youthful Hezekiah.

1. *Sweeping Changes*

It took a good deal of nerve to step up to the driver's seat and throw the entire machinery "in reverse." Hezekiah acted with a courageous enthusiasm born of God that caused him to institute sweeping changes everywhere. Vineyards, towers, pools, aqueducts, fortifications, reservoirs, and buildings were greatly improved.

He won the love and admiration of his people as he sought to do everything possible for their welfare. He had as his close, intimate friend and adviser the great statesman, Isaiah. No king ever had a better counselor than this great prophet.

2. The Temple Restored

The doors of the Temple were soon opened. Priests, Levites, workmen, and architects were called back to work again. Ahaz had made it practically impossible for the worship of Jehovah to be carried on. It was a big task to clear away the "filthiness" of the house. The sacred vessels were found, cleansed, sanctified, and brought back to their places.

When the house was fit for worship again, there was a joyful day of dedication and thanksgiving. Offerings were brought, hearts rejoiced, songs were sung, and the people were happy in the worship of Jehovah. Hezekiah, who led in the service, seemed to be happier than any other in the entire group.

3. The Passover Observed

Following the great service, Hezekiah led his people in the observance of the Passover. The people of Judah and also the people of the Northern Kingdom were invited to this celebration. Many laughed and mocked when the messengers came to them with the royal invitation, but a goodly number answered the call and came to the solemn meeting.

When the people came together, they became conscious of a great number of idols, altars, images, and

idol furniture that did not fit into the picture. Led by
Hezekiah, they fell upon these evidences of idolatry and
dumped the broken fragments into the field. Even the
great altar, erected by Ahaz after his trip to meet Tiglath
at Damascus, was demolished and carried out by the
zealous followers of Hezekiah.

It was a happy group that came back to the solemn
assembly for the sacred observance. They were singing,
shouting, and worshiping God as they did his will. We
may be sure that Isaiah and Micah were responsible for
a great deal of this zeal for Jehovah. They must have
been the moving force behind Hezekiah to stir up so
much enthusiasm for Jehovah.

4. Sennacherib Faced

When Hezekiah came face to face with Sennacherib,
in 701 B.C., his faith was sorely tested. The great warrior
had run over all of Palestine, had defeated Egypt, and
was at that moment ready to attack and destroy Jerusalem. It seemed foolish to try to withstand such an invader. His army was invincible. The immediate doom of
Jerusalem seemed inevitable.

It was in this trying hour that Hezekiah showed a
daring faith that had not been equaled by any king before him. He was so convinced that Jehovah was going
to defend his city that he boldly defied the great Assyrian
army. It looked like suicide, but it was the way to victory.
God delivered his city and his kingdom. Sennacherib
suffered the most serious defeat of his career when he
found 185,000 dead on the field as a result of Jehovah's
hand. He went back to Nineveh to spend the rest of his
life. He did not come against Jerusalem again.

5. *The Influence of Isaiah*

We must pause a moment to give credit to that mighty statesman, Isaiah, who spoke with such conviction and effectiveness that Hezekiah and his associates were compelled to believe. Isaiah was the greatest man alive in his day. Jehovah honored him and his city by predicting the certain overthrow of the proud Assyrian who was to be led back to his land with a hook in his nose.

III. MICAH, THE YOUNG DEMOCRAT

Micah was called of God to preach his word to the sinning people during the days of Jotham. His ministry was in the land of Judah during the reigns of Jotham, Ahaz, and Hezekiah. Isaiah was his great contemporary. God raised up Micah to champion the cause of the poor and oppressed. He was primarily concerned with social justice and religious duty. The nobles were getting richer by making the poor people poorer. Courts were corrupt and the poor could not hope for justice.

Micah must have taken an active part in the reformation under Hezekiah. His strong preaching prepared the way for the king's reform measures. He was rough, crude, pointed, and vigorous in his preaching. He was greatly concerned for the welfare of his poor, defenseless neighbors. His righteous indignation blazed forth in stinging words of reproof and ringing challenges to repent. He was as fearless as he was direct.

1. *Doom Promised*

Graphically Micah pictured the coming of an invader who would carry the people away into exile. God was bringing this army to cause trouble and correction. Captivity was a definite step in God's program for his Chosen People.

Micah was certain that he could explain the call to go into exile. It was not because of an arbitrary ruling of a heartless God, but because of specific sins of the people of Judah. They had made it necessary.

2. Greed and Corruption Denounced

With fierceness Micah attacked the "land-grabber" who lay awake at night making plans to catch the poor victims on the morrow. Early in the morning he made his way to evict the poor owner of the land. He then claimed it as his own, while the poor man was left without a home.

The greedy creditor who plucked the cloak from the back of the poor man and who drove helpless women and children from their homes was the target for one of the prophet's strongest sermons.

The judges, governors, and rulers were attacked because of their love of bribes and because they were unwilling to render a decision except as it would provide spoil for them. In Micah 3:2-3, he accused these men of being cannibals, killing, cooking, and eating his people.

Prophets and priests were as false as anyone else. The preachers delivered soft messages to please the people who paid the salary.

In fact, all the people were false, and Micah could find no one in whom he could confide. The religious leaders were opposed to him, and the rulers certainly did not appreciate his stinging words. He was battling bravely and hopelessly to make men turn and come back to God.

3. God's Program Announced

Micah was permitted to see God's program for his Chosen People. It had the following steps in it: anguish, captivity, exile, punishment, years of purging, a glorious return, and the proclamation through the redeemed remnant of salvation for the world.

Micah was certain of the judgment that was to come to people who deserved it. He was just as certain that beyond the dark clouds a new day of restoration would bring an opportunity for the evangelization of the world. The city must fall, the people must suffer in order that the new day of rejoicing might be made possible. The people had gone so far in sin that reformation was out of the question until captivity brought it about.

Taking the long look, the prophet was able to look far beyond the smoking ruins of the city and the piteous cries of the exiles. He saw the mighty hand of God working out his plan and purpose.

Jerusalem was to fall, but the beautiful little city of Bethlehem was to continue through the centuries until one day One would come to bring peace, healing, salvation, and joy to his people. Micah saw the Messiah coming, not from the great city, but from the remote place where the poor peasant farmers and shepherds lived. It was Micah who gave the directions that guided the Wise Men when they came to find the Child. Seven centuries meant nothing to the Spirit who could reveal to Micah the birthplace of the Saviour.

Micah also gave to the world a picture of the effects of

that Messiah's reign when universal peace would come. It is to be a glorious day when men are willing to abdicate the throne to the Prince of peace who has a right to reign.

4. Jehovah's Lawsuit Set Forth

In chapters 6 and 7, Micah gave a statement of essential religion. He was talking to men who thought of God as an unlimited despot whose wrathful spirit and thirst for blood must be satisfied with costly gifts and bloody sacrifices. Micah brought to them in one brief statement a summary of the messages of Amos, Hosea, and Isaiah. Each of these prophets had emphasized an essential feature of true religion. The keynote of Amos' teaching was *justice*. Hosea struck the richer, deeper note of *love*. Isaiah called for a *reverent walk* in fellowship with the majestic Sovereign who was yearning for fellowship.

This magnificent statement was truly a foregleam of the message of Jesus who came to make this vital requirement of essential religion clear to men and to constrain his followers to present themselves according to the requirements in the Sermon on the Mount.

IV. ISAIAH, THE STATESMAN PROPHET

The greatest man alive in that eighth century was Isaiah, the prophet of God. He began his ministry about 740 B.C., and was still preaching at the close of the century. For forty years he served God in his native city, Jerusalem. Under Jotham, Ahaz, and Hezekiah, he preached the word of Jehovah. As a statesman and adviser of kings, Isaiah has had few, if any, equals. As a faithful, courageous, effective interpreter of God's Word, he stands at the top. His was a marvelous work.

1. *The Divine Call*

Isaiah's call came in the year that king Uzziah died (740 B.C.). It was a never-to-be-forgotten experience. As a young man he saw the Lord sitting upon a throne. During all the years of Isaiah's life he was never able to get away from that experience. It was to him the most significant moment of his life, just as Paul always looked back to the experience on the Damascus road as the turning point in his life.

In that call Isaiah saw Jehovah, saw himself as a sinner, saw the needy world crying out for a guide and Redeemer, and he willingly volunteered to go as a humble preacher for his God. The commission was a startling one and too heavy for human shoulders to carry. Jehovah would uphold and bless his prophet and make his message effective.

2. *Under Ahaz*

From that moment Isaiah was under the divine direction and must do God's will. During the days of Jotham he was getting his bearing and beginning his ministry. When Ahaz came to the throne, Isaiah had a difficult task. The king was not at all interested in Jehovah. He could not be bothered by anything like religion. He became openly hostile to anyone who sought to promulgate the teachings of Jehovah.

When Rezin of Syria and Pekah of Israel came against Judah, it caused a panic in the small brain of Ahaz. He was incapable of a great faith in the God who had done so many things for his people. He probably despised Isaiah and Micah. He knew that his army was weak, his water supply inadequate, and defeat inevitable. What could a mere man do under such circumstances? Ahaz proceeded to tremble and to call on Tiglath-pileser of Assyria to come to his rescue.

Isaiah had a faith in God that was big enough to cause him to advise Ahaz to lean heavily on God and fear no man. The prophet was well aware of the dire consequences of an alliance with the cruel Assyrians. His advice to the godless young king was ignored. The fatal step was taken, and Isaiah left to go on with his preaching to a people who refused to listen to him, just as their king had done. They were rapidly following a wicked king away from God.

3. Advice Concerning Egypt.

When the Assyrian yoke became heavy upon their shoulders, the politicians advised turning away from Assyria and calling upon Egypt to help them. The young Hezekiah, who hated to see his people suffer under the Assyrians, seems to have agreed with the Egyptian party in their proposal. Isaiah came into the breach at once with his powerful challenge to trust God and remain loyal to the covenant already made. He told them of the strength of Sennacherib's army that would soon be hurled into the West and of the utter futility of trusting on Egypt to save them. It would be a suicidal policy of bad politics and bad religion. If they could only trust God, they might rest securely in his own gracious hands.

4. The Crisis

When Sennacherib finally came against the rebellious nations in Palestine, he swept all before him as he marched triumphantly on through the land. Finally, Jerusalem was the only city in the land that was left. Messengers came to demand the surrender of the city, since nothing could prevent its capture and destruction. It was Isaiah the statesman who stood in the breach and deliberately assured Hezekiah and the people that Jehovah would save his city, and that no harm would come to anyone in that secure spot.

How could the city be saved? Apparently nothing could possibly stop the proud conqueror. All the armies combined could be brushed aside as so many flies. Yet Isaiah stood forth as God's spokesman to guarantee safety. That faith in God was the secret of it all. He had God's word for it and he knew that no harm could come to the city. His faith was vindicated when 185,000 soldiers were left dead upon the ground and the enemy was utterly routed without one arrow falling in the city. God's great prophet had more wisdom than all the other statesmen.

V. PICTURES OF THE MESSIAH

As great as Isaiah was in the nation to counsel, advise, and encourage, he was even greater as an interpreter of God's will for the future. He preached great messages and controlled the policies of state, but he was also able as a prophet of God to pull aside the screen and show us glimpses of the coming Messiah.

In the book which bears his name, Isaiah has given us some of these pictures. (See chapters 2, 4, 7, 9, 11, 16, 32, 42, 49, 50, 52, 53, and 61). Even though he wrote seven hundred years before the coming of the Christ, he was able to put down for us some words and descriptions that only one who was inspired could reveal. The marvel of predictive prophecy is too great for us except as we see the God back of the human prophet. When we see the divine Author we need not doubt anything that has been put down for us.

In the early chapters Isaiah revealed the Messiah as Immanuel—"God with us"—and then as "Wonderful, Counsellor, Mighty God, Everlasting Father, Prince of Peace" (Isa. 9:6 ASV). In chapter 11 it is shown that that same Person is to be a king from the stock of Jesse. He is to be divinely equipped and will rule and judge with supernatural skill, while peace will come as one of the results of his reign.

When we come to the section of Isaiah called the "Book of Comfort" (chapters 40 to 66) we face the other great pictures of the Anointed of God. The four "Servant Poems" (42, 49, 50, and 52:13 to 53:12) are classics that command our best thinking. In them the prophet has pictured the Servant's call, his gentleness, his perseverance, his twofold mission to Jew and Gentile, his preparation, his patience and endurance, and his exaltation following his humiliation and suffering.

In the great fifty-third chapter that Suffering One is pictured as taking the sins of others and voluntarily suffering that the debt might be paid. He gladly takes the place of the guilty one and dies in his stead.

"Surely he hath borne our griefs, and carried our sorrows; yet we did esteem him stricken, smitten of God, and afflicted. But he was wounded for our transgressions, he was bruised for our iniquities; the chastisement of our peace was upon him; and with his stripes we are healed."

Though innocent as a lamb, the Suffering Servant died

without resistance as a part of the infinite plan of God. In his death he was among the wicked ones, and his grave was with the rich. (Compare Matt. 27:38, 57–60). How could this prophet speak such words and paint such pictures? He was under the control of the Spirit who revealed to him the pictures.

Isaiah was the greatest of the long line of prophets who heard God's call and came to the people with the divine message. His influence can never be fully measured. God called him, prepared him, inspired him, and used him to do his will.

FOR CLASS DISCUSSION AND FURTHER STUDY

1. List the four great prophets of the eighth century B.C. Find and read some characteristic statements from each. You may begin with the following:

    Amos 3:3; 5:4,14–15, 24; 6:1; 7:7–8,14; 8:11; 9:14–15.
    Hosea 2:19–20; 3:4–5; 4:6; 6:3; 10:12; 11:1,3,8; 14:4, 9.
    Isaiah 1:18,25–27; 2:2; 3:10; 4:2; 7:14; 9:6–7; 10: 20–22; 11:9; 12:2; 25:4,8–9; 26:3–4; 28:16; 33:6; 40:8,28–31; 42:4; 53:1–12; 55:10–11.
    Micah 3:8,12; 4:1–4; 5:2; 6:8; 7:18–20.

2. In the book of Isaiah, find and read the pictures of Messiah in the chapters mentioned in this text. Read also the four "Servant Poems."

3. Cite specific instances to show how the prophets influenced kings and, through them, the civil and religious life of the people. How did the situation in the eighth century differ from our emphasis on the separation of church and state. In what ways should church leaders today exercise an influence similar to that of the prophets?

CHAPTER 7

MANASSEH, JOSIAH, AND JEREMIAH

**2 Kings 21–25; 2 Chronicles 33–36;
Jeremiah 1–52**

IT WAS A SAD DAY for Jerusalem when Isaiah, Hezekiah, and Micah passed off the scene of action. They were the three men who for a quarter of a century had kept the people in line for the worship of Jehovah. Even with them the country had been made to suffer severely under the invasion of Sennacherib. It seems that the miraculous deliverance from the threatened disaster would have made it impossible for the people to turn away from Jehovah.

I. THE WICKED MANASSEH

Hezekiah's twelve-year-old son succeeded to the throne of Judah in 698 B.C. He was the worst of all the long line of kings, and remained on the throne longer than any of them. The heathen party took immediate control. Tradition tells us that Isaiah was sawed asunder by the order of Manasseh. It was a tragic period for the followers of Jehovah.

All known heathen cults and customs were introduced,

and the impure rites were set up by the official order. Much innocent blood was shed while the people hid themselves from the cruel monarch. Manasseh's long reign of fifty-five years practically sealed the doom of the land. Even good Josiah and the great prophet Jeremiah could not avert the judgment that must come. They could not hope to wean the people away from the sinful practices into which they had been led. It would take a miracle to extricate the people from the depths. After that wild half-century, captivity was inevitable.

Manasseh continued his loyalty to Assyria, paying the heavy tribute regularly. It was a heavy load for his people to carry, but it was the only way to continue as a nation.

II. THE GOOD KING JOSIAH

At the age of eight, Josiah came to the throne of Judah. With such a background it seemed impossible to expect a good reign, but the boy became the best ruler after Hezekiah. His father Amon and his grandfather Manasseh were as bad as the worst. For over fifty years the nation had been steeped in sin and heathen worship. How could a mere boy amount to anything?

Evidently Josiah had some good advisers who loved Jehovah and were courageous enough to break away from the established order of things and help lead the people back to God. The priest Hilkiah must have been the good influence in the life of this boy, who was still too young for the Junior department.

As a boy Josiah began seeking the Lord and learning of him as the Guide of his way. It was not long until he was leading a group in the destruction of idols, heathen altars, images, and other furniture of false worship.

Later in his reign Josiah set about repairing the Temple. It evidently needed a great deal of work to make it presentable, as it had suffered seriously during the years of Manasseh and Amon. Shaphan and Hilkiah were in active charge of the work. After a great deal of rubbish had been removed, the priest found an ancient copy of the Torah of Moses. Shaphan read it and took it to the king. Each of the three men was alarmed and excited over the remarkable find. They had never seen such a book before. They recognized it at once as being the book of the Law given by Moses.

The king was shocked because of the realization of the divine wrath upon him and upon his people. The book revealed enough to cause him to tear his clothing into shreds and prostrate himself upon the ground. He could not be certain of any way of escape, for God's threats were severe.

The king sent the book with a special delegation to the prophetess Huldah for her word concerning it. She informed them that the threats would all be fulfilled and that the people must suffer as a result of their sins. Because of the goodness of Josiah, the nation would be spared during his days. Terrible days were coming for the land. Defeat, exile, tragedy, suffering, and punishment were near.

The people were called together from all parts of the realm to hear the reading of this book of the covenant that had been found. All the laws, promises, and threats that the book contained were read to the people. While still deeply affected by the message, they were called upon to ratify the Mosaic law as the law of the land. They took a solemn oath to that effect.

Immediately the people were led forth to destroy every idolatrous altar and symbol that existed in the city and its environs. They moved under the direct orders of Jehovah to break down and demolish every vestige of heathen worship. They went as far afield as Bethel and the land of Israel. Josiah willingly made a covenant with Jehovah "to walk after Jehovah, and to keep his commandments, and his testimonies, and his statutes, with all his heart, and with all his soul, to perform the words of the covenant that were written in this book" (2 Chron. 34:31 ASV). It was great to see the young king and his people stand together in a solemn pledge to carry out all of the requirements of the old covenant. It was a sweeping reform that extended throughout the entire length of the land and carried out every vestige of heathenism.

Josiah was probably ably assisted by Zephaniah and Jeremiah. They became great prophets who were closely associated with Josiah, and we may be reasonably certain of their help in this crisis. Zephaniah was a powerful preacher of the word of the Lord.

In 612 B.C., Nineveh, the capital of Assyria, fell before the combined attacks of Medes, Babylonians, and Scythians. The remnant of the inhabitants fled to Haran for their last stand. Pharaoh Neco (Jer. 46:2) of Egypt started across the land to help his friend, the king of Assyria. At Megiddo, he was attacked by Josiah. Just why Josiah was foolish enough to make such a move we can never know. It was suicide. In the battle the good king Josiah was mortally wounded. It was a tragic day for Judah. The sun set on the kingdom of Judah when Josiah died. It was only a few steps to the end.

Jehoahaz, his son, was placed on the throne by the people, who hoped to continue the same fine policies, but he lasted only three months, when Pharaoh Neco came back and put Jehoiakim in his place to do the bidding of Egypt.

III. THE END OF THE KINGDOM

After the death of Josiah, the end came rapidly. The people followed Jehoiakim back into the worst sins, and the prophets of Jehovah had a hard time. Jeremiah suffered under him.

Nebuchadnezzar, the new king of Babylon, soon put an end to the Assyrian and Egyptian power. It was easy for him to come against Jerusalem in 605 B.C., and in 598 B.C., taking the treasures and the best of the young men of the city. Daniel was among the captives in 605 B.C., and Ezekiel was carried away in 598 B.C.

The city was left with Zedekiah acting as king under Babylonian control. In 587 B.C., he revolted again, depending on Egypt for assistance. When Nebuchadnezzar came with his army he finished his task completely. The walls were broken down, the houses were burned, the Temple was completely demolished, many were killed and the others taken away in chains to Babylon.

It was a tragic day for the city of David and for the glorious Temple of God. The fate predicted by the prophets had come upon it. In Isaiah's day the city was miraculously spared because God had something further in store for it. It fell in Jeremiah's day because the people had sinned away every right they had to divine protection.

Zedekiah escaped but was captured in the valley. Brought before the king, he watched the execution of his sons, and then had his own eyes burned out before the long journey to Babylon began.

The kingdom of Judah, after three hundred and forty-four years of existence, was finally crushed. During these years, nineteen kings had sat on the throne. Each of them was a direct descendant of David. Zedekiah was the last of the line. From that moment there would be no kingdom of Judah as such. After seventy years some of the survivors would come back, but not to establish a kingdom.

IV. The Ministry of Jeremiah

Jeremiah was born in Anathoth, a small village just outside Jerusalem. The son of a priestly family, he was definitely interested in the Temple and its services. Josiah was trying to bring the people back to the worship of Jehovah.

1. *His Call*

Jeremiah's call to prophetic service came in 626 B.C., while he was still a boy. He shrank from the task which the Lord laid upon him, because he recognized his own limitations and also saw what tremendous odds he would have to face in Jerusalem. It was a burden calculated to cause a strong man to stagger. How could a mere lad do it?

Jehovah did not lose patience with the youngster, but replied with tenderness, sympathy, and promise. The divine presence was assured for every difficult task. His weakness would only add to his effectiveness because it would allow Jehovah to carry out his plans without interference. He said to Jeremiah: "I formed thee . . . I knew thee . . . I sanctified thee . . . I have appointed thee . . . I am with thee" (Jer. 1:5,8). The God who knew all about Jeremiah's weakness had appointed him to be Jehovah's personal representative to the people.

2. *His Early Ministry*

During the days of Josiah, this young prophet developed into a mighty preacher. Jerusalem was the scene of his labors. Zephaniah and his aunt Huldah were his associates in the ministry. They all had a part in the reform movement of the king, and together they were able to turn the tide of religious loyalty back to Jehovah. The finding of the book of the Law and its meaningful words must have made a profound impression on Jeremiah.

When Josiah was mortally wounded at Megiddo, it practically broke the prophet's heart. His best friend was gone. It would not be safe for him to preach again in the land, for every official would oppose him to the end of the kingdom.

3. *Under Jehoiakim*

Jeremiah was so courageous and fearless in his preaching that the prophets and priests and people were soon clamoring for his head. Jehoiakim was his bitter enemy, too. To add to his misery, he soon became conscious of the appalling fact that Judah's idolatry was incurable. His prayers for his people could not be answered. They had sinned, and punishment alone could be their portion.

Jeremiah was not allowed the comfort and solace of a

wife to help him in his work. Forbidden to marry, he had to carry on alone in the midst of his distressing conditions. His own people of Anathoth conspired against him. It seemed to his sensitive soul that everyone was against him. It served to drive him back to his God, from whom he derived his strength.

His roll was taken, read, cut into shreds, and burned in the fire by an infuriated king who opposed him at every turn. Under God's direction, Jeremiah set to work to write it again.

Arrested, beaten, and put in the stocks by the priest, Jeremiah became deeply discouraged and sought to quit preaching. He tells us that such a course was impossible, for there was a fire shut up in his bones that caused him to go on preaching at whatever cost. The poor fellow was carrying a load too heavy for mortal man. He was able to go on only as Jehovah came to his rescue and helped him.

When Nebuchadnezzar, the great Babylonian conqueror, appeared in 605 B.C., Jeremiah began to preach the unpopular doctrine of submission. He predicted the complete overthrow of the city and seventy years of exile. His countrymen called him a traitor for such talk. In the face of hatred and fierce opposition, Jeremiah continued to preach that message from God. As the divine spokesman, he was given insight into the plan of God for his people and was able to interpret coming events.

4. *Under Zedekiah*

Jeremiah breathed easier when Jehoiakim passed away, but there was not much relief from his successor or from Zedekiah, the last king. The people were bitter in their opposition, and it was very difficult for Zedekiah to show any mercy toward the preacher, even if he had been disposed to do it.

The false prophets contended that no harm could come to the city and that the captives taken away in 605 B.C. and 598 B.C. would soon be on their way home again. It was necessary for the true prophet to continue his unpopular announcement of the fall of the city and a long exile.

When Nebuchadnezzar's army encamped against the city, Jeremiah was in an embarrassing position. Since he was in direct communication with God, he knew just what was certain to happen. Without hesitation, Jeremiah urged Zedekiah and his group to submit to the invader and save the city. This advice branded him as a traitor, and he was pronounced a dangerous man to have in the midst of discouraged soldiers. In order that Jeremiah might not do any further damage, they arrested him and threw him into a pit to die.

The king needed Jeremiah to give counsel concerning the future of his city, and so he was taken to a clean room in the king's own house where he was kept a prisoner.

In desperation, the people came to the king demanding the life of the old prophet. Zedekiah was too weak to assert his own rights, and so Jeremiah was turned over to the fury of the mob. Instead of murdering him outright, they threw him into another dungeon where death would be certain. They had murder in their hearts.

Jeremiah had one good friend at court who gained permission to save the preacher from his precarious position.

The Ethiopian used thirty men to draw Jeremiah from his muddy grave. He was restored to his place in the house of the king, where he remained until the capture of the city.

Jerusalem finally could stand the siege no longer. There was no food, and the water supply was about exhausted. Zedekiah and his family group escaped under the wall as the enemy gained entrance from the front. There followed a scene of carnage, destruction, and disaster. Houses and palaces were burned. The Temple was completely destroyed. The sacred vessels were taken away with the other treasures. The walls were knocked down, and the people who were not slaughtered were made prisoners to start the long journey to Babylon.

5. *Jeremiah, a Privileged Character*

Evidently Nebuzaradan, the commanding officer, had heard of the stand that Jeremiah had taken throughout the siege. At any rate, orders were given that the prophet was to be spared and brought to headquarters as a special prisoner. Jeremiah was allowed to choose between going to Babylon with the captives or remaining in Jerusalem to encourage and strengthen the group left to carry on under Gedaliah, the newly appointed governor of Palestine. He chose to remain in his old city as Jehovah's representative among the bad group left to inhabit the land. He thus escaped the humiliation and hardships of an enforced march to Babylon.

The prophet's work with the new governor was far from easy. The neighboring people were not anxious to see a strong band of people in the vicinity of Jerusalem. They hired an assassin to get rid of Gedaliah so that they could have control of the land. Immediately there was a panic among the people. They were afraid to remain in Jerusalem, for the Babylonians might punish them severely for upsetting the established government. In desperation, they decided to go to Egypt. They took the helpless old prophet with them into the land he hated so much. Jeremiah had escaped one exile only to be led into another one.

In Egypt, God still used the old preacher to proclaim his message to the Jews who assembled about him. Jeremiah announced to them that Nebuchadnezzar, from whom they had fled, would soon come into Egypt to capture the land and set up his throne on the ruins of an Egyptian civilization. This prophecy was quickly fulfilled.

The Jews in Egypt were guilty of several forms of idolatry. Jeremiah denounced the burning of incense to the "queen of heaven." They were so completely given over to idolatrous worship that his preaching was fruitless. He must have died of a broken heart without ever going back to the land he loved so dearly. One Jewish tradition claims that Jeremiah was stoned to death by his own people who were tired of his attacks upon them. He gave them the best that he could for nearly half a century. They refused to hearken to him.

6. *An Estimate of Jeremiah*

How shall we judge such a character? For half a century Jeremiah preached for God among people who despised him, feared him, hated him, persecuted him, and refused to listen to his words. They called him a traitor. God forbade him to pray for the sparing of the people whom he loved better than his life (Jer. 7:16–20). He was forced constantly to announce exile for the people and to fight on when he was assured that victory was impossible. Jeremiah hated idolatry, and gave his life fighting manfully against it. Was his life a failure?

Jeremiah preached to people who were going into exile; and those people opened their eyes one day to realize that the preacher was right, that God was able to carry out his promises and threats.

Jeremiah preached two definite doctrines that helped prepare the way for the new day when God would be more real and personal. He emphasized the doctrine of individual responsibility and that of the new covenant. The way was being prepared for the New Testament doctrine of spirituality and individualism. Jeremiah was prepared for such a message because of his intimate touch with God. During those lonely years when practically everybody was hostile to him and the future looked dark, the preacher was forced to lean heavily upon his God. God became a real friend who upheld him and sustained him through the darkest hours.

FOR CLASS DISCUSSION AND FURTHER STUDY

1. Explain the sentence "Manasseh's long reign of fifty-five years practically sealed the doom of the land."
2. How do you account for the fact that a good king like Hezekiah had a wicked son like Manasseh?
3. How do you explain the fact that Josiah, the righteous boy king, succeeded a wicked father and grandfather?
4. Do you think Jeremiah's ministry was considered a success by the people of his day? In what specific ways did he help to prepare the way for New Testament teaching?

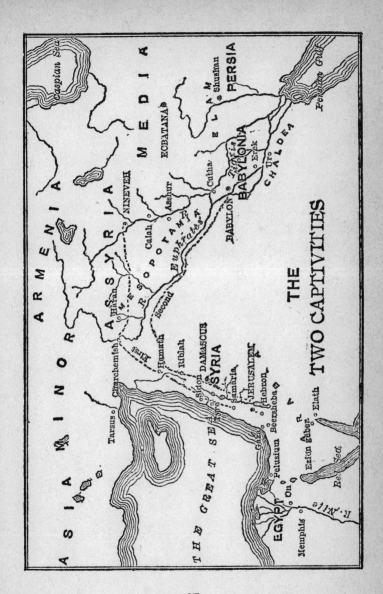

THE TWO CAPTIVITIES

97

CHAPTER 8

8

EZEKIEL AND DANIEL

Ezekiel 1–48; Daniel 1–6

TWO PROPHETS, Ezekiel and Daniel, ministered in Babylon to the people of Judah.

I. THE EXILES IN BABYLONIA

The great host of Jewish captives taken away by the order of Nebuchadnezzar in 587 B.C. took up their residence by the waters of Babylon. They were not scattered among other peoples as the prisoners from the ten tribes of the Northern Kingdom seem to have been, but were allowed to remain in a compact group so that they could keep up their old family ties and enjoy a measure of autonomy.

During the first few years the Jewish captives were deluded with the hope of a speedy return to the old home. They could not believe that the city of Jerusalem would fall. The news of the fatal catastrophe was a blow too heavy for even their stout hearts. When they recovered from the first shock, they settled down to make themselves at home and wait for the long days to drag by. They were in colonies in one of the most fertile plains of the world with plenty of water for irrigation.

There was plenty of time for reflection and meditation.

They thought back to the messages of the prophets and the threats that had been unheeded. They realized now that their God was speaking through these men his own unchanging word concerning his people. They were able to take to heart the stern messages of these men of God.

II. EZEKIEL, THE PREACHER

Ezekiel was taken to Babylon in 598 B.C. along with a great host of the best residents of Jerusalem. He was a member of the family of Zadok and in the regular order of the priesthood. His stay in Babylonia must have been a very unhappy one as he watched daily for news of a return.

Ezekiel's good friend, Jeremiah, was preaching in Jerusalem. King Jehoiachin was in prison in Babylon. Zedekiah was on the tottering throne at Jerusalem. Daniel was taking his place as a wise officer in the affairs of Babylon. Hosts of Ezekiel's friends were sitting by the "Great Canal" (river Chebar) weeping, wailing, and lamenting. It was a dark hour for the energetic, ambitious, patriotic, young priest.

1. His Call to Preach

In this tragic situation the hand of the Lord came upon Ezekiel with such force that it shocked him. Gradually he became conscious of the fact that he was being called to preach for his God. It was the divine challenge to service.

In a vision Ezekiel saw Jehovah, and the sight of the divine Being caused him to fall upon his face. Then he heard the voice from the throne of God calling him to become a prophet to the exiles. He knew that he was being singled out to do a specific work for God. He felt the power of God opening his eyes and his heart. The voice charged him to be brave, submissive, and obedient in the full performance of the arduous task.

In the heat of the never-to-be-forgotten experience, Ezekiel was offered the roll of the book and commanded to eat it. It was a sweet morsel for him as he obediently accepted the challenge to be God's spokesman to deliver faithfully every word received from God for the people. He was made to understand that he should be made strong to endure the hardest toil for his Master. Ezekiel described himself as being gripped by the Almighty with such power that he could never forget the strange feeling. God's hand was truly upon him.

Ezekiel tells us that, under the spell of that experience, he went forth to preach to the captives by the river. Instead of preaching to them immediately, he sat down for seven days side by side with the weeping exiles. In that way he was enabled to know the burdens, the sorrows, the doubts, the fears, the hopes, and aims of the people to whom he was to minister. He was better able to preach after those days of preparation. If we could only see the point of view of the other fellow, we could do a great deal more in helping him in his difficulty. That principle in operation would help in every phase of life. It was the principle which Jesus put into operation.

Ezekiel was conscious of the fearful responsibility that rested upon him as Jehovah's representative to man. He was made to believe that he was being held responsible for the faithful deliverance of the message to every person who could be reached with it. We do not wonder that Ezekiel was exceptionally effective as a prophet.

2. *His Early Ministry*

For six years Ezekiel preached to people who were expecting Jerusalem to continue to stand. They were counting on returning to the old home to enjoy the blessings of the Temple worship again. They could not believe that the sacred sanctuary could be destroyed. Jeremiah was trying to convince the people in Jerusalem that the city must be captured, and Ezekiel was seeking to do the same thing for the exiles. False hopes had to be dealt with in each instance.

In a vision, Ezekiel was carried to Jerusalem for an inspection tour of that wicked city. He was convinced that the amount of wickedness found there demanded punishment. He saw that Jehovah was determined to blot out the sins of the land and take his people away into a place of purging. It was necessary for Ezekiel to be stern and uncompromising in his messages of doom. The people must know God's will and recognize his hand in the events that were to be seen. The prophet's work was not popular, but it would bear fruit.

In order that Ezekiel might teach his people the proper way to accept the inevitable news of the fall of Jerusalem, the prophet was informed that on the morrow his wife would die. He was commanded to face that grief with dry eyes and without lamentation. With a strange display of courage, the prophet met the emergency and explained to his people the coming catastrophe that they were to face.

Ezekiel had a more difficult task in convincing the people that the calamity was due to their sins. Such sins had made suffering necessary. He wanted them to begin reaping the benefit to be derived from the exile. They must be willing to bow to the will of God, accept his correction, and look forward to the future when the seventy years would end and the arm of God would be thrust forth to lead his own people back home.

3. *His Later Ministry*

After the fall of Jerusalem, in 587 B.C., Ezekiel had a much larger congregation, and the tone of his message was different. He was now the faithful pastor of his flock and sought to bring them messages of hope, cheer, and encouragement. It was his privilege to interpret the acts of God to a bewildered and discouraged group. They must be led to see that the exile was merely an interruption in the career of the nation and not a disruption of God's plans.

Ezekiel would not compromise with sin, but he always held out hope for the sinner. He pictured each man as having the power to be righteous or wicked, irrespective of hereditary predisposition. In each case the individual was the master of his own destiny and wholly responsible for his acts. Each man was free and also responsible. Man was not bound by any conduct of his ancestors or by his own past conduct. Heredity and habit were both powerless, if the individual chose to exercise his own will. It was a new note and a hopeful one for the exiles.

The prophet represented God as a loving One standing ready for any repentant child to come home. He did not rejoice in the death of anyone, but yearned for the wayward child to come back to God.

Ezekiel was primarily interested in the full restoration of the Jewish nation. He thought of the exile as God's instrument of chastening. His people were really in the grave, but the dry bones would live and the nation would come forth from the grave. When the elders suggested the building of a temple on Babylonian soil, Ezekiel opposed it with all his might. He did not want anything to hinder the complete restoration of the nation to the old land. "For in my holy mountain, in the mountain of the height of Israel, saith the Lord Jehovah, . . . there will I require your offerings" (Ezek. 20:40 ASV).

Ezekiel foresaw the collection and return of the captives from all the lands and the new settlement upon the mountain at Jerusalem. With painstaking detail he laid out the plan of the new building as well as the lines of the future policy of the nation. He made it clear that the one condition of the future glory was national penitence, a new heart, and a new spirit. God would provide the new heart and spirit.

One of the most hopeful pictures of the entire Old Testament was presented by Ezekiel in chapter forty-seven. The life-giving stream flowing from the altar in the Temple increases in volume as it flows eastward, transforming the Dead Sea into a picture of life, health, and prosperity. Wherever the water goes, life comes immediately. Even the death of the Dead Sea area is driven away.

III. Daniel, the Statesman

When Nebuchadnezzar returned from Jerusalem in 605 B.C., he brought back some of the finest young students of the land. Among these was the young prince Daniel. It was a serious blow to the boy to be dragged away from his people and his native city to become a prisoner in the foreign capital. It was about eighteen years before the final destruction of Jerusalem, when the rest of the people were taken to Babylon.

1. *The Young Student Prince*

We are told concerning the young captives that they were "of the seed royal and of the nobles; youths in whom was no blemish, but well-favored, and skilful in all wisdom, and endued with knowledge, and understanding science, and such as had ability to stand in the king's palace" (Dan. 1:3–4 ASV). Daniel and his friends certainly came to the court of Nebuchadnezzar highly recommended. They were select youngsters who gave promise of fine future development. The king was happy to honor them with a great opportunity.

It was easy for Daniel and his friends to pass the entrance examination that admitted them into the select group of those who were being trained for Babylon's "wise men." They were qualified to take their places among the best of the realm. In this school they were given the finest advantages that were available for the best education. They were signally honored.

2. *Meeting Temptation*

In the new life at the court, Daniel was immediately faced with powerful temptations. It would have been easy to conform to the practices and customs of a pagan court. Jerusalem and Jehovah could well be forgotten. A new life could begin now with all the old restraints gone. Daniel wanted to be popular with the king, the other students, and with his teachers. He was under strict discipline, and was to obey all orders of the king. It certainly seemed that it was time to fall in line with the ways of Babylon and conform his walk to the accepted formula of the new home. The good food must have appealed to the growing boy. In short, the temptation to do as all the others about him was probably very strong. The challenge to "dare to be different" was not such an attractive one under the existing circumstances.

3. *A Daring Resolve*

"Daniel purposed in his heart that he would not defile himself with the king's dainties" (Dan. 1:8 ASV). Daniel was one young student who refused to allow himself to be driven into something that would injure him, even though all the others were willing to go that way. We admire one who has the nerve to stand up for his convictions and refuse to be defiled. Daniel had been building character for years. In this testing time he proved that he was made of the right material.

Daniel knew that the food and the drink were not according to the law of Moses, and that they would render him less efficient. He knew that he would be going contrary to God's will for his life were he to break over and submit to the new commands. Daniel wanted to be physically strong, mentally alert, and spiritually clean. His purpose saved him untold agony, sure defeat, and endless obscurity. Because he was willing to pay the price, his name has come down to us clear, shining, illustrious, and will be revered to the end of time.

4. *An Honor Graduate*

When the officer agreed to the proposed test suggested by Daniel, the victory was really won. At the end of the time set for the trial, it was easy to see that Daniel and his friends were doing better than the other students. God was helping his children even though they were in a strange land.

When graduation day came, these four students who had refused "to defile themselves" stood so far ahead of the other members of the class that there was no question of their superiority. Daniel took his place easily as the "valedictorian." How did he do it? How could a mere change of diet work such a miracle? We find the answer in Daniel 1:17. "God gave them knowledge and skill in all learning and wisdom: and Daniel had understanding in all visions and dreams." Jehovah was willing to honor one who was willing to honor him. Daniel was the best in his group because God chose to give him wisdom, insight, understanding, and knowledge. God chose to honor him because he was strong enough to put out the things that displeased God and to put in the things that pleased him.

It is refreshing to read the account of such a victory. There are so many defeats, failures, and dwarfs in the world that we are always thrilled when we find one who is willing to let God have his way in every step of the way. Paul said: "We are more than conquerors through him that loved us" (Rom. 8:37). The way to triumph is the way of obedience, decision, faith in him, and a resolute purpose to let him do the leading. Victory is certain for such a youngster every time.

5. *A Victorious Life*

Following his student days, Daniel became an honored member of the organization of "wise men." He con-

tinued throughout a long life to exhibit more wisdom
than anyone else in the realm. Under God he was able
to interpret dreams and messages that were wholly unin-
telligible to all others. Kings listened to him, heeded his
words, rewarded him profusely, and honored him as an
outstanding leader among them.

Nebuchadnezzar needed help in a trying hour. Of his
wise men, all but Daniel failed him. It was a fine thing to
see him come from God's presence to reveal the hidden
secrets of God's message to the great monarch. As a result of his rare contribution, Daniel was elevated to a
place of honor and authority among the people. In that
capacity he was able to be of great help to his brethren
who were in exile. He did his part as a wise ruler and
statesman, while Ezekiel preached to the people. The
way was being prepared for the coming of the great
Cyrus and for the return of the captives. God was using
all these various events and persons to effect his purpose
and to make ready for the restoration of the remnant.

When Cyrus came into the land to put an end to the
Chaldean Empire, Belshazzar was seated upon the
throne. (Nabonidus, his father, was the king, but Belshazzar seems to have been in control of the affairs of
state and was called "king"). Daniel was an old man at
the time but, when all others failed to decipher and interpret the message written on the wall of the palace, he
was called in to make clear to Belshazzar the meaning.
Faithfully and courageously the aged prophet delivered
God's message to the drunken king. Daniel was easily
the greatest man in the kingdom.

Cyrus must have listened to the suggestions of the
wise old Jewish statesman when he took over the land.

We may be sure that it was Jehovah's way of influencing the Persian king to restore his people to Jerusalem.

The same God who had given Daniel wisdom and uncanny insight came in his later years to supply the courage, faith, and confidence necessary to face the hungry lions without flinching. God convinced his prophet that there was safety in a lion's den when the divine hand controlled the jaws of the beasts. It was a glorious experience in the life of God's man.

Daniel lived in Babylon throughout the entire seventy years of the captivity. His contribution to the life of God's chosen people cannot be measured. He served valiantly, faithfully, and wisely during seventy turbulent years. His was a life wholly committed to God. Fear, cowardice, impurity, intemperance, failure, defeat had no place in his life. He was a conqueror with God.

FOR CLASS DISCUSSION AND FURTHER STUDY

1. Consider the location and circumstances in which Ezekiel prophesied and see if you can decide why he used so much symbolism in his writing. Ask class members to do some research and report on the characteristics and uses of apocryphal literature in the Bible.
2. Discuss the missionary message in Ezekiel 47.
3. List the kings who were directly influenced by Daniel, and evaluate his contribution to the carrying forward of the purpose of God.

CHAPTER 9

9

AFTER THE EXILE

Ezra 1–10; Nehemiah 1–8; Haggai 1–2;
Zechariah 1–6; Malachi 1–4

IT TOOK SEVENTY YEARS to prepare the hearts of the people for the restoration to their own land. During these weary years the people suffered in a strange land because they had been unwilling to listen to God's words. They had plenty of time for reflection and for repentance. They could draw nigh unto God and come to know him better while the storms were beating upon them. Hope for a better day kept them looking forward and made them trust in the One who could bring it to pass.

We cannot overestimate the work of Daniel and Ezekiel during that period of chastening. They were God's instruments to reveal his will to the people and to guide them toward that hour when release would come. They were God's men for a crisis to interpret the will and purpose of God to a bewildered group of captives.

I. GOD USES CYRUS

While Nabonidus looked after his gods and Belshazzar gave a great banquet, the city of Babylon fell under the relentless attack of the great Persian conqueror. Cyrus was invincible. His armies swept on throughout

111

the world, making opposition useless wherever he went.

Just as he had used Nebuchadnezzar to bring his people into captivity, Jehovah used Cyrus to get them started on the way home again.

Isaiah spoke of Cyrus as God's anointed. He was in truth the chosen one of God to release the captives and speed them on their way. In his early days in Babylon Cyrus began the policy of restoring war prisoners to their homes. He was anxious to win the love and gratitude of his new subjects. By sending the Jews back to Palestine, he could establish a stronghold on the direct route to Egypt. He had everything to gain and nothing to lose by the venture.

We must not lose sight of the divine side of the undertaking, for God was using the great king to carry out his purpose. Daniel was one of the most influential men of the entire city, and must have been used by God to suggest the new idea to Cyrus.

An official proclamation was made that all the Jews might return at once to Jerusalem. Cyrus went so far as to bring out all the golden vessels which Nebuchadnezzar had taken from the Temple and deliver them into the hands of the leaders. The Persian king became so enthusiastic over the new venture that we are tempted to think of him as a worshiper of Jehovah. He probably showed more interest in the God of the Jews because Jehovah was working in his heart at that time to bring about his purposes for the return.

Cyrus urged all the Jews to go on this pilgrimage. If they were unable to make the journey, he showed a willingness to help them. If they were so situated in "business" that they did not care to go back to a barren land, he urged them to make substantial contributions to the expenses of the journey. We cannot estimate the help that Cyrus made possible.

II. THE RETURN TO JERUSALEM

In the year 535 B.C., a caravan of fifty thousand persons left Babylon to make the journey to Jerusalem. They were led by Sheshbazzar or by Zerubbabel. (It is possible that these were two names for the same person. It is more probable that Sheshbazzar, the prince of Judah, was governor under Cyrus and that Zerubbabel was appointed by Darius). The new governor of the land of Judah went forth with royal authority to take complete charge of the new home. The sacred vessels and the generous gifts were transported safely across the dangerous stretches of the journey. It must have been a happy band that finally came in sight of the Sacred City. It had been over fifty years since the city was destroyed. Now God's chosen people were coming home again. God's promises were fulfilled.

III. THE TEMPLE REBUILT

It will always remain a mystery to us just why these zealous people waited fifteen years to build God's house. That had been the one great desire all through the long night of captivity. Prophet, priest, and people had cried out for a temple. It seems that nothing could have stopped them from putting God's house back upon the sacred hill.

In 520 B.C., when Darius came upon the scene as the Persian emperor, they were still without a temple. They had built ceiled houses for themselves, but God did not have a house. They had tried, but the difficulties and obstacles were too great for them. They were not willing to pay the price to have the Temple again.

It was not until Haggai and Zechariah were called of God to preach that the people were challenged to rise up and build. These two prophets came with a burning message. God was not to be defeated simply because his people had been unwilling to undertake great things. It is always God's supreme opportunity when men fail. It is then that he is able to come in with a definite challenge to go forward in a great way.

These two preachers came with fire in their hearts to call the people to listen to divine reasoning. God was concerned because his people were more interested in material things than in things of the Spirit. The people were hiding behind a very pious excuse, "It is not the time." They had fooled themselves into believing that they must wait for a later time to undertake a work for God. It was the devil's favorite excuse.

The prophets' call to these people was one of consecration to duty. They could prove their loyalty to God only by putting forth all their energy in actual work. There could be no other adequate expression of their love. When they could get to work they might expect the outpouring of God's Spirit in a mighty way so that material blessings and spiritual gifts would come to them.

Obedience (Haggai 1:12a), fear (12b), encouragement (13), assistance (14a), and work (14b–15), are the outstanding words of that challenge. The good preaching of these men bore immediate fruit. The material was quickly gathered, and the house was built. The willing workers seemed to be inspired by the realization that

God was in the very midst. They worked with energy and enthusiasm.

Even though the new structure failed to measure up to the fine building that the older men had known, they were encouraged by the promise that God would pour out such rich blessings upon it that the glory of the new house would far surpass the old. Jehovah would be a close, personal, intimate Friend who would be available and adequate for every moment and every emergency.

After four years of diligent work, the house was completed and dedicated. It was a glorious victory, and the cause of Jehovah was again prospering in the land. Haggai and Zechariah had preached, and Zerubbabel and Joshua had led the people in the work. This quartet of worthy men may well be remembered and honored by us. They heard the voice of God and obeyed that challenge fully. God is always honored by such obedience. His work is accomplished through such loyal followers.

IV. Ezra, the Scribe

After the completion of the Temple in 516 B.C., we do not get another glimpse into the city of Jerusalem until the coming of Ezra in 458 B.C. What happened during all those years? How did God's people fare? Who preached to them? Who served as priest? These nearly sixty years are hidden from us.

Ezra had spent many years in studying, copying, and preserving the books of the Hebrew writers. He seems to have been at the head of the company of scribes who had entrusted to them the sacred rolls. These books were to be kept and finally incorporated into the canon. It was a great service that these men did for God and men. The rolls that were written before the fall of Jerusalem must have been guarded closely and sacredly as the captives were driven away into captivity.

Ezra was a priest who could trace his line all the way back to Aaron. Since he lived in Babylon, he was not needed as a priest, and it had been the natural step for him to become an active scribe.

In 458 B.C., Ezra felt the call of God to make the journey to Jerusalem. King Artaxerxes seemed to be enthusiastic over the new venture. He ordered his people to provide generously from the royal treasury that Ezra might be thoroughly equipped and that needed supplies be available for the Temple worship.

The chief men of the colony of exiles were invited to go along with Ezra. A large number of the best citizens responded. After earnest prayer, the party set out upon the long journey without human protection. It was a great display of faith that God would see the expedition through the dangerous hazards of the way. Ezra claimed that he was ashamed to ask for a guard after he had been so strong in his declaration that God was able to help him.

After about four months of hard marching over the same journey that Abraham made, they finally arrived in Jerusalem. The rich treasures and the people had been protected through all the dangers. God had kept his promise, and Ezra's faith had been honored. He was God's man for a serious crisis, and he was found faithful to the end.

Ezra's place as an interpreter of God's Word to the people was an important one. He was probably the best qualified of all the people on earth to do that work of an interpreter. His long years of study and meditation now bore fruit.

The people were taught the words and the message of "the Law, the Prophets, and the Writings" (as they were called by the Jewish people). As the people came to understand God's Word for them, they were better able to live worthy lives. As a man of commanding character, Ezra was to impress himself mightily upon the people of Jerusalem and become the leader of the new Jewish state and the real founder of Judaism. He was God's great man for a great task.

V. NEHEMIAH, THE BUILDER

About fourteen years after Ezra's journey to Jerusalem, the call came to Nehemiah to leave his work as cupbearer to King Artaxerxes and go to Jerusalem to rebuild the walls. Nehemiah was greatly distressed to learn of the serious plight of the people who had returned. They needed a wall to make life at all bearable.

His sadness manifested itself and the king noticed the symptoms. When the request was made, Artaxerxes gladly gave Nehemiah a leave of absence from his work, full authority to rebuild the wall, authority to rule over the people of the city, letters to the governors on the way to insure safe passage, and a special letter to the keeper of the king's forest reservation to secure timber for the buildings and the walls. It was a generous grant. God worked through a heathen king to make his work possible.

Nehemiah's first task was to survey the work before him and to convince the people that it could be done. He convinced them that the task could be accomplished since Artaxerxes was lending his authority and resources, and God was promising to make it possible. They agreed heartily to his call and began the work with enthusiasm.

In spite of serious opposition by Sanballat, Tobiah, and Geshem, the work moved forward. Nehemiah dismissed these "pious piddlers" with the reminder that he was working under orders from "the God of heaven." They continued to trouble and try to trap him that the work might be hindered, but Nehemiah plunged steadily on in the path of duty.

Each person in the city was convinced of his own responsibility in carrying out the work. With enthusiasm and zeal they built the walls; it was a mighty enterprise. At the end of fifty-two days, the work was finished and the gates were in their places. After one hundred and forty years, the Sacred City had walls around her again. The citadel was built and guards were placed to make the city safe from troublesome enemies.

Following the completion of the building operations, the people came together to praise God and learn the meaning of his Word. Nehemiah was as deeply interested in the new revival as he had been in the building of the walls. Ezra joined him in reading and interpreting the Word. The people were strangely moved and gave themselves to earnest effort to understand and obey the commands of God. The revival culminated in the renewal of the covenant of Jehovah.

After a brief visit to Babylon, Nehemiah returned to Jerusalem to cleanse the Temple, to set up true worship, to insist on the bringing of tithes, and to demand the observance of God's commands. He was a reformer who took God's commands literally and sought to lift the people to the divine standard for them.

What were some characteristics of Nehemiah which help to explain his success?

1. Nehemiah was a man who had faith in God. He knew God and understood something of his absolute power. It did not seem to occur to him that one of God's enterprises could fail. He trusted the Lord implicitly and was willing to follow all the way.

2. Nehemiah was a man of courage. In the face of hard work, enemies, difficulties, and danger, he continued the work. His courage was born of conscious sincerity and of conscious union with his God. He knew that he was right, and he knew that the eternal God was backing the work with his resources. We do not wonder that Nehemiah displayed such unusual courage! Fear had no power over him.

3. Nehemiah was willing to work. In seeking for the secrets of his success, we can be certain of this one. His big task could not have been accomplished by sending orders from his hotel suite. He was in the midst of his men, giving his best all the time.

4. Nehemiah was a man of perseverance. It must have been inspiring to watch a man who would not quit. Steadfastness was his crowning virtue. To him, a difficulty was only a glorious opportunity. Ridicule was a spur to make bigger investments of time and energy. In the face of all the things calculated to cause him to quit, he went forward to the finish line.

5. Nehemiah was a man of prayer. We miss the best part of his life if we fail to see him in prayer. The real secret lies in the closet. He was great because he knew

God in prayer. His faith was strong because of the assurance that came from the secret place. He was able to do a mighty work because he was in tune with God and received divine orders daily.

6. Nehemiah was a man of wisdom. In looking upon a man who showed extraordinary wisdom, we must not lose sight of the fact that he was constantly under the guiding touch of God and consequently was able to make many wise decisions. If we examine the career of Nehemiah, we find many evidences of a superior intelligence that seemed to weigh the evidence and arrive at conclusions in such a way as to leave no doubt of his wisdom. His dealings with his enemies reveal an uncanny power of insight into their plots and schemes. He was God's man, endowed, chosen, inspired, trained, equipped, guided, and consecrated to finish the work given him by Jehovah.

VI. MALACHI, THE REFORMER

This vigorous reformer began his ministry about 432 B.C., and aided Nehemiah in his work of cleaning up the conditions in Jerusalem. There were many abuses in the land. The people were in open sin, the priests were corrupt, temple worship was a disgrace, while a godless sort of indifference had settled upon the land. Blind and crippled animals were offered upon the altar. The men were divorcing their own Jewish wives and marrying heathen women. They were unwilling to bring the tithe to God.

Malachi came to remind the people of God's love. It is significant that the Old Testament closes with such a statement as: "I have loved you" (Mal. 1:2). The charge brought against the inhabitants of Jerusalem was that they had disregarded that love and had robbed God of the love and loyalty that was due him as well as the life of service that should grow out of that love and loyalty. The prophet announced certain judgment upon the priests, people, and the land.

Following the specific charges and the definite prediction of doom, the prophet exhorted the people to return to God, bring in tithes, and prove God to see the rich blessings that he would pour out upon the land.

The rich promises that Malachi made are exceptionally interesting in view of the black sins of the people. He represented a God who still loved and who was willing to forgive his sinful people. He was authorized to promise material blessings, spiritual blessings, the good will of neighboring people, and the coming of "the Sun of righteousness . . . with healing in his wings" (Mal. 4:2).

Malachi believed in a God who demanded social righteousness and who was willing to bestow rich gifts upon his people according to their response to his call to them. Obedient loyalty would bring the richest blessings.

VII. After Malachi

It was approximately four hundred years before the coming of Christ. Who lived during these years? What happened? How did they get along without preachers? It is a fascinating story, but not one for us to study here. (Read *Josephus* for a thorough treatment.)

The Jews continued under the Persian rule until about 331 B. C. Then they suffered under Alexander the Great for years before the Ptolemies of Egypt took possession

of them. In 198 B. C., the rule passed over into the hands
of Antiochus the Great of Syria. It was not until 167 B. C.
that the yoke of Syria was broken by Mattathias and his
brave sons. Native kings ruled in Jerusalem until 63 B. C.,
when Pompey captured the city. Herod the Great ruled
from 37 B.C. until after the birth of Jesus.

During these years there was practically no preaching.
Judaism hardened into pharasaic legalism. The stage
was finally set for the coming of the King of kings who
came to fulfil prophecy. In the fulness of time, this Redeemer came to bring the knowledge of the Father to
men and to be his salvation to all.

FOR CLASS DISCUSSION AND FURTHER STUDY

1. Why did God permit his people to remain so long as exiles in
   Babylon?
2. Explain why God would refer to a heathen king like Cyrus as
   "his anointed" (Isa. 45:1).
3. Summarize the distinctive contributions of each of the following in carrying out God's purpose: Zerubbabel, Ezra, Nehemiah, Malachi.

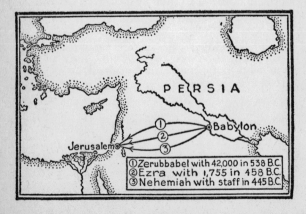

① Zerubbabel with 42,000 in 538 B.C.
② Ezra with 1,755 in 458 B.C.
③ Nehemiah with staff in 445 B.C.

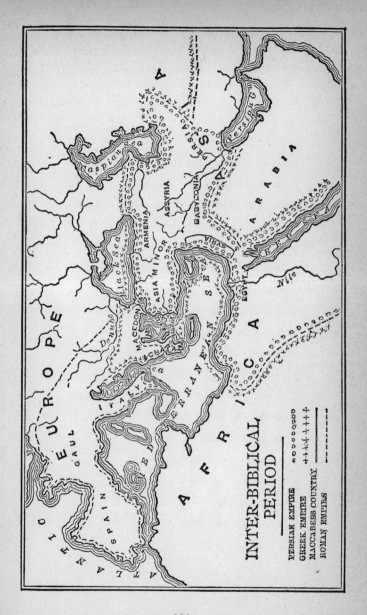

INTER-BIBLICAL
PERIOD

PERSIAN EMPIRE o o o o o o o o
GREEK EMPIRE +-+-+-+-+-+-+-+-+
MACCABEES COUNTRY ——————
ROMAN EMPIRE — — — — —

Bibliography

SAMPEY, *The Heart of the Old Testament.*

KIRKPATRICK, *The Doctrine of the Prophets.*

WARD, *Portraits of the Prophets.*

DAHL, *The Heroes of Israel's Golden Age.*

BAYNES, *Israel Among the Nations.*

MARGOLIS, *History of the Jewish People.*

SMITH, *The Book of the Twelve Prophets.*

SMITH, *Isaiah* (2 volumes).

SMITH, *Jeremiah.*

WALKER, *Men Unafraid.*

ROBINSON, *The Twelve Minor Prophets.*

MERRILL, *Prophets of the Dawn.*

GORDON, *The Prophets of the Old Testament.*

GORDON, *The Rebel Prophet.*

WELCH, *Jeremiah.*

JEFFERSON, *Cardinal Ideas of Jeremiah.*

JEFFERSON, *Cardinal Ideas of Isaiah.*

WEATHERSPOON, *The Book We Teach.*

YATES, *Preaching from the Prophets.*

Questions for Written Work

CHAPTER 1

1. Describe Solomon's auspicious beginning.
2. What serious mistakes did Solomon make?
3. State the facts in Jeroboam's early life.
4. Name some causes of the division.

CHAPTER 2

5. State some strong points and some weak points in Jeroboam's policies.
6. What did Asa do for his land?
7. Name an effective thing that Jehoshaphat did to rid his land of ignorance.
8. What was Omri's most outstanding contribution?

CHAPTER 3

9. Describe the contest on Mount Carmel. What did Elijah expect following the victory?
10. Tell of the challenge that God had for Elijah on Horeb.
11. Why did Ahab need a sermon at Naboth's vineyard?
12. What work did Elisha accomplish?

CHAPTER 4

13. How did Jehu stamp out Baalism?
14. Describe the reforms of Jehoash.
15. Compare the reigns of Uzziah and Jeroboam II.
16. What is the main lesson we may learn from the book of Jonah?

CHAPTER 5

17. State the main teachings of Amos.
18. Describe the times of Hosea.
19. What new message did Hosea gain from his tragic experience?

CHAPTER 6

20. Name the four great prophets of the eighth century.
21. Give some of the leading events in the career of Hezekiah.
22. What was God's program for Judah as stated by Micah?
23. How did Isaiah show himself a great statesman?

CHAPTER 7

24. What did Manasseh do to corrupt Judah?
25. Describe the finding of the Law during the reign of Josiah and its effects upon the people.
26. Give the main facts in the fall of Jerusalem.
27. What hardships did Jeremiah have to endure?

CHAPTER 8

28. Give the events in the call and preparation of Ezekiel.
29. What was Ezekiel's advice to the captives?
30. Can you give Daniel's reasons for "daring to be different"?

CHAPTER 9

31. What part did Cyrus play in the return of the Jews to their own land?
32. What arguments did Haggai and Zechariah use in their preaching?
33. Give the principal contribution of Ezra.
34. Describe the building of the walls of Jerusalem. State some of the secrets of the success of Nehemiah.
35. What was Malachi's contribution to his people?

Date